"What struck me most about 'It's Nev _____
redefines value. She shows that success in ....,.....
financial rewards. Her insights on building strong teams and motivating people through culture are truly game-changing."

– **Jon Gordon**, 17x best-selling author of *The Carpenter* and *The Power of Positive Leadership*

"I've known and respected Michelle Simms for many years. Her new book, 'It's Never About the Money,' is a firsthand testament that hard work and treating people the right way will ultimately translate into both business and personal success. Creating a flourishing homebuilding business during one of our country's worst economic downturns was certainly noteworthy, but achieving this as a young female in a male-dominated industry was downright courageous. Michelle outlines a roadmap in this book that managers in any industry can apply and quickly reap rewards. With her real-life experiences and the establishment of a Signature Culture, Michelle discloses the recipe to her secret sauce for success."

– **John Anthony**, Regional Executive and Executive Vice President, Fidelity Bank

"Good job! I could definitely relate to many of the performance motivator descriptions, particularly in my current Change Champion role. I had just performed the slightly depressing math that my 1-hour of expert witness testimony at $650 was equivalent to selling more than 13 books. I have already had requests for the less expensive desk version, but the original goal of being a durable field guide was met! At this point, I am more about spreading the message than the actual form in which that message is delivered."

– **Derek A. Hodgin**, PE, RBEC, CCCA, CXLT, F-IIBEC, CPSI

"Having known Michelle Simms for many years, I can say firsthand that she is a powerhouse of wisdom and leadership, and her book, 'It's Never About the Money,' reflects her incredible journey. Michelle's approach to leadership and people management is revolutionary, yet deeply personal. She doesn't just focus on success; she teaches how to build it from the inside out, with relationships, culture, and authentic

leadership as the cornerstones. Her stories and insights will challenge the way you think about motivating and leading teams. This is a must-read for anyone serious about creating a lasting impact."

– **Erica Lockwood**, Managing Director, Executive Partner, Director of Diversity, Equity & Inclusion

"Michelle Simms has crafted a compelling and insightful guide for leaders seeking to build high-performing teams. 'It's Never About the Money' offers practical strategies and valuable insights for attracting, retaining, and motivating top talent. Her unique blend of systematic thinking and genuine human connection resonates deeply. This book is a must-read for anyone aspiring to create a thriving and fulfilling workplace culture."

– **Rich Nowalk**, Chief Strategy Officer, Opex Technologies

"Michelle Simms' Performance Motivator™ System is an innovative, smart, systematic approach to investing in the heart and soul of every organization—its people. Dig in with Michelle, and I promise you will gain paramount and shocking revelations about yourself and learn how to foster meaningful and productive connections among your team members. Be prepared for super-charged success in all things, personal and professional."

– **Laurie Ford**, Principal, LOMONACO INVESTMENTS

"The Six Performance Motivators are a game changer! You can take personality tests and better understand how your team thinks, but this is different. It's about what drives your team to perform at their best. When you know that, you can place them in the right roles and challenge them in a way that is truly fulfilling for them and impactful for your company."

– **Melissa Langdale**, President and COO, The Mortgage Collaborative

It's Never About the Money

It's Never About the Money

Activating the Performance Motivator™ System to Attract, Retain, and Motivate People

Michelle Simms-Reiter

Published by Game Changer Publishing

Paperback ISBN: 978-1-966659-08-2
Hardcover ISBN: 978-1-965653-62-3
Digital ISBN: 978-1-965653-63-0

www.GameChangerPublishing.com

It's Never About the Money

Activating the Performance Motivator™ System
to Attract, Retain, and Motivate People

Michelle Simms-Reiter

www.GameChangerPublishing.com

Foreword

For over three decades, I have had the privilege of working in an industry that is about far more than bricks and mortar. As Executive Chairman for D.R. Horton, I have witnessed our company prevail through some of the most turbulent circumstances, thanks to the dedication and determination of our employees. Our founder, and my dear friend, Don Horton, recognized early on the importance of maintaining the culture and motivation surrounding the people in our company – the "Horton Family." He put the growth of his employees, the work environment, and company culture at the forefront of business decisions, propelling D.R. Horton into the respected organization it is today. Even in his passing, we carry forward his philosophy of serving our people to achieve our highest goals.

My connection with Michelle began over six years ago when D.R. Horton acquired Terramor Homes. Since then, I have watched her excel professionally and take on multiple leadership roles in various aspects of her life. It's gratifying to see Michelle share her knowledge in this book, providing guidance for those seeking professional growth. At the core of It's Never About the Money lies the underlying principle that any company's greatest resource is its people. Michelle highlights that a key component of effective leadership is understanding how to best serve employees. Many leaders assume that financial incentives are the primary driver of motivation, yet Michelle challenges and widens that perspective. She gives practical advice, real-life stories and actionable strategies to provide a structure for growing a successful business capable of reaching its goals. This book is a testament to the principles that make leaders – and companies – endure.

– David Auld, Chairman of the Board of D.R. Horton, Inc.

SUCCESS SEEKER

CHANGE CHAMPION

IMPACT PLAYER

PERFORMANCE MOTIVATOR™

STRUCTURE WI...

BOUNDARY BALANCER

TRIBE THINKER

Prologue

The contract has been signed. The due diligence is well underway. Our executive team is working hard – day and night- to meet all the requirements and deadlines to close in a timely manner.

This was the biggest closing transaction we have ever had. I never could have imagined this day was possible. Back on Christmas Eve, December 1999, at just 24 years old, I was finally offered my dream job with a small, locally owned home-building company. I spent several years ahead learning everything I could and soaking it all up. Little did I know that the small company had already been purchased by one of the largest home-building companies in the nation before I even started.

Now, it's fall of 2018, nearly 20 years later, and I am at the seat of the ownership, offering our company up for sale to that same exact company where it all started.

But we have an important test to pass next. Mr Don Horton, the founder and head of the largest home-building company in the nation, net worth in excess of $5.9 billion, insists on meeting each of the owners of any company he plans to purchase and fold into the carefully built culture he has been building since 1978.

Based on his request, we will be meeting him at our local Cracker Barrel restaurant for breakfast on a Saturday morning at 7 a.m. before he begins his market tour of all his communities. Yes, you read that correctly—Cracker Barrel restaurant, and yes, 7 a.m. on Saturday morning.

"Intimidated" was an understatement for me. However, it was quickly replaced with ease and confidence as we sat and drank coffee with him that morning, talking about people, culture and community. He has since passed; (1950-2024) may he be resting in peace. He was one of the most down-to-earth, genuine and extremely intelligent leaders you could ever meet. People were important to him. He wanted assurances that the leaders of the companies he purchased were just as committed to people, culture, and true care for others as he taught and led himself. While we may have been very different in some of our accomplishments, this was something we knew we had in common. And for that reason, our acquisition was a big success.

I will never forget that day in Cracker Barrel and the lessons that I learned from him. It doesn't matter how much you achieve and accomplish, and it doesn't matter how much money you have. Working at 7 a.m. on a Saturday morning comes with the territory of building a business, no matter what size. Caring for people is never beneath anyone, and neither is having breakfast at Cracker Barrel!

Table of Contents

Introduction

It's Never About the Money.

"It," for the purposes of this book, refers to the workplace: companies, employees, and the other ingredients, plus the recipe it takes to create success.

Throughout history, money has been just one representation of value among many options used to exchange products and services. Today, it has become the one and only thing anyone thinks about when it comes to representing value in trade for anything and everything. Over time, in our evolved and prosperous economic world, we've forgotten about the long list of other tremendously valuable options and possibilities. Money is used—mistakenly, in most cases—as a band-aid to fix problems. Money has often become the inaccurate focal point in discussions about compensation packages, hiring agreements, and business partnerships, overshadowing the original motivations and goals that brought everyone to the table.

Whether you are the CEO, an executive leader, a business owner, a middle manager, or just have dreams of becoming a leader in business in any capacity one day, this book is for you. I wrote it not only as a reminder of all the other possibilities but also to challenge the conventional way of thinking. When it comes to creating a culture of success and maximizing the potential and capabilities of people and companies of any size, regardless of your position, it is almost never about the money.

MOST LEADERS WANT TO SOLVE THESE PROBLEMS.
THIS IS THE ANSWER.

- **Attracting and retaining top talent:** This allows your business to thrive, reduces turnover, saves money, saves time, and makes your life easier, so you can focus on your real job instead of constantly hiring and training people.
- **Being proactive rather than reactive:** When someone says they are leaving, you won't be faced with throwing more money at the problem in an attempt to fix it—saving money.
- **Increased loyalty:** Fewer people will seek opportunities outside the company when they are satisfied where they are. This creates more loyal followers, allows you to be seen as a high-quality asset to the organization, and maximizes your own value—leading to more opportunities and greater satisfaction.
- **Higher morale:** This results in better quality work, improved job satisfaction, higher customer satisfaction scores, better problem-solving and collaboration, and leaders who create a smoothly running organization that stands out above the competition.

Until recently, I believed that my approach to successfully leading teams, creating positive cultures, and achieving success—as evidenced by the many awards we won and the financial gains we realized—resulted from an intuitive, almost accidental method. I assumed it was simply common sense, something that everyone possessed. But I've since come to realize it wasn't common sense at all. Instead, it was the culmination of many lessons I learned, the mentors I had, and the experiences, successes, and failures that evolved into a set of ingredients. Over the past few years, I took the time to break down these ingredients into a recipe that can be replicated time and again. Anyone can do it. Anyone can learn and practice gathering these ingredients and following these recipes to develop an intuitive, common-sense approach as well. Common sense? Yes. Simple? Yes. Intuitive? With practice… Yes.

I started a home-building company in 2007. If you remember 2007, you might recall it was in the midst of the Great Recession. A record number of companies were closing and going bankrupt, but very few were starting. To those watching from afar, this seemed like the definition of insanity.

Ironically, I learned that things were not about money at all during a time when we had no money. I didn't have deep pockets to hire great people. I didn't have the cash flow to retain A-players, and I didn't have the financial guarantees to motivate talent during the worst of times and in extremely challenging market conditions.

If you've ever faced the challenges of recruiting, motivating, and retaining talent—especially top talent—I understand your struggles. I've been in your shoes and empathize deeply.

Despite these challenges, as a female leader in a male-dominated industry, I prevailed. We built an incredible team and, in just over ten years, created one of the largest and most successful companies in our MSA (Metropolitan Statistical Area). We went from building and selling 36 homes in our first year to consistently selling 300 homes per year as a small, local builder with revenues of $85 million annually. We positioned ourselves to be sought after and acquired by the largest home-building company in the nation. It was a tremendous success, achieved by an incredible team.

Since then, I've continued building partnerships and successful companies with others, helping them create strong cultures and leaders and developing strategies for business success. This remains a driving and fulfilling force for me.

While my business focus has been on developing great leaders and cultures, the purpose of this book is to have the same powerful impact on any culture and for any manager, leader, or business owner who reads it and implements these simple, straightforward strategies.

You will walk away with the key ingredients to building your most successful culture and a step-by-step recipe for maximizing your potential and success in business. The challenges of recruiting, motivating, and leading top talent to achieve your business goals will no longer be the obstacles holding you back.

My hope is that, by implementing these practices and making them part of your company's intuitive culture, you will create a top-of-market, exclusive culture and reputation—regardless of your size or industry. You will become the most sought-after leader with a loyal following and create a workplace filled with people who love working for you and appreciate contributing to the company for the reasons they are passionate about. If I could do this in the worst of times, with limited resources, as a female in a traditionally male-dominated industry, then you absolutely can achieve even more.

This book is structured to introduce the proven method I have successfully implemented over the past 25 years, which I teach to others every day and still use myself—the Performance Motivator™ System. However, to properly implement it, there are important steps that must first be taken to lay the groundwork and allow for my approach to be applied in the most powerful and effective way.

Think of it like building a home. Every home is unique. The way it looks, feels and smells, the decor, and the accessories—each unique. Your company is no different—no two are the same… nor would you want them to be.

This diagram represents the entire "**Performance Motivator™ System.**" It is the construction method that creates a company that is your **Signature Culture.**" Your Signature Culture represents everything you stand for, represented in every aspect of your company, including what your team and your clients can see and everything they can't. What's aesthetically pleasing to the senses, and also the level of quality of everything that is behind the walls holding it up, each defines your company, just like the construction of a home.

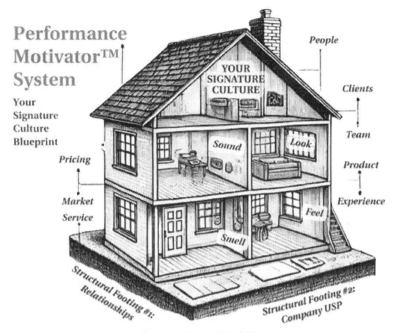

Foundation of Stability

You must start with a strong foundation, which requires two essential elements: proper site preparation and high-quality materials. Without stable soil and proper grading, the foundation can shift or crack, jeopardizing the entire structure. Similarly, using reinforced concrete and steel ensures the foundation can withstand pressure and environmental challenges over time. Both elements are critical—without them, even the most well-designed home won't stand the test of time. A **Foundation of Stability** is the critical start for any company.

As part of the company's **Foundation of Stability**, I will build upon it to outline the **Two Structural Footings** that allowed me to create my unique culture to stand out in the marketplace, creating my beautiful, unique, special company. I'll show you how you can do the same things. I'll be expanding on these critical **Structural Footings, #1: Relationships and #2: Company USP**, to reflect how they are each individually important structural components that must be in place before we begin the framing and construction of the other elements.

Once you have these components solidly in place, we can build our beautiful company, your **Signature Culture**, to create an incredible and personalized culture, create high-quality products, run efficiently, and develop your best team, clients, and experience to make it a beautiful, special, and unique place to be. To do this, I will use my own story as a case study and set the tone to construct those two imperative structural footings.

Next, I will show you how to utilize the **Performance Motivator™ System**, the approach that provides you with the exact steps to take to implement it, along with specific, real-life case study examples for each. This is the key to creating all the bells and whistles that define the feel, the look, the sound, the smell, and the overall vibe of your company. Your *Product, People, Team, Pricing, Clients, Experience,* and *Service* will create the results that you desire that define the **Signature Culture** of your company.

Finally, in the examples I will outline ahead, you may see yourself, your co-workers, your peers, and even your own leaders and mentors. Each of the stories is true, with the identifying details and names changed to respect their privacy. If you think you recognize yourself in any of these stories, just know that there are hundreds of others who likely also identify with the same exact stories. This will make it an interesting and thought-provoking approach that, once you know, you can never "*un-know.*" It will become an unforgettable perspective that will change how you meet and talk to people, making it so much more interesting and fun.

Before we begin, let's address the elephant in the room. I made a bold statement by naming this book, *It's Never About the Money.* I'm betting some of you read that title and believe it, are skeptical about what I have to say, or at least thought, *Well, sometimes it is about the money.* If you're one of those people, I appreciate that you've read this far. I'm not naïve enough to think that this concept will sway everyone just because of the title. But I have proven this approach to be true countless times in my 25-plus year career, with story after story of evidence. I believe in this approach with every fiber of my being. It's not a statement I make lightly or just for the impact of the title, although that's also true. Let's get right to it in the first chapter so we can set aside doubt and skepticism and focus on putting these approaches into practice to help you attract, motivate, and retain the talent you need on your team. Let's get started by discussing why *it's never about the money.*

CHAPTER 1

Money: The Elephant in the Room

The title of this book focuses on the topic of money and confronts us with the dilemma of "the money discussion." So, let's address it upfront before we dive into the stories. If you are one of the skeptics reading this book, I see you, I hear you, and I understand what you're thinking. I know because, over the years, as I've developed and taught these concepts, I've encountered many others who share your belief that everything boils down to money—that people are primarily motivated by it and that money solves most problems, if not all of them. Many successful and wealthy mentors, clients, and leaders have shared this belief with me, drawing on their own experiences where money seemed to be the solution to their problems. And, for them, it often has been, in the short term.

But then, I come along and share the stories and challenges that I will present to you in this book. And guess what? Every single time, they have been able to recall examples from their own careers where the concepts I propose could have made a difference. They recognize situations where, had they addressed things differently with my approach, they could have saved time, trouble, and, most importantly, *money* for their companies. EVERY. SINGLE. TIME.

The obvious caveat here is Maslow's hierarchy of needs. Every human must first satisfy their basic survival needs—breathing, water, food, sleep, shelter, and clothing. While money isn't required to create these things, it is often the simplest way to acquire them. For this reason, money can be a necessity in fulfilling these basic needs. However, I assume that for most readers of this book, these fundamental requirements have been met or can be met. Therefore, the message of this book applies beyond that point.

Let's start by answering this question:

If you were offered another job tomorrow with the same compensation package, benefits, and overall similar key metrics, would you leave your current company to work for them? If not, why would you stay?

Taking a few moments to reflect on this question and answer it, as well as the "why" behind it, will set the tone for our discussion about money and the overall premise of this book. It lays the foundation on which these lessons and practices can be based.

Simply put, money is the socially accepted currency of trade for goods and services. It represents one form of measurement, no different from a measuring tape or a measuring cup. Money is necessary for basic survival and thriving in any first-world economy, but it is not synonymous with value. Volunteering, charity, and many other goodwill activities are also measures of value. Value is subjective, perceived differently by each person, and evolves over time, whereas money is merely a medium of exchange.

For most people, I would argue that money is not the primary driving factor in their decision-making. Many other motivations and reasons influence people's choices. Money is often mistaken for the means to something far more desirable. When we think about money, we think about what we want it to buy us. Is it freedom? Is it fame, friendships, and belonging? Is it love and acceptance? Is it cars, homes, and material possessions? If so, why do we want these things? What will having them make us feel we have achieved? What does it mean about us if we possess them? Or if we don't? These questions allow us to dig deeper into the underlying emotions that drive our desire for money. Isn't it interesting to realize that there's always something else that powerfully drives the claim that money is the ultimate goal? As leaders, understanding this can help us use it more effectively to motivate others.

Money is not the only measure of achievement, reward, or fulfillment. And because it is merely a symbol—whether in the form of paper, metals, or numbers on a screen, used for society's agreed-upon exchange of goods and services—it cannot, on its own, create any of the above-mentioned things. So, the real question is: How do the things money can buy achieve this for someone?

I have managed many people throughout my career and have connections with highly successful entrepreneurs, business owners, and high-level corporate executives. Some of them already embrace these concepts in their leadership style and the cultures they've created. They believe in these principles at a core level through their leadership journeys and career experiences. Yet, many others do not. Their first response is, "I don't believe any of this—people are all about the money, and that's the most important thing to them. If they can get a higher-paying job, they'll leave, and they don't care much (or at all) about anything else."

Maybe that's true sometimes. I'm willing to concede that there can be situations and circumstances where this could be true.

Now, allow me to challenge the thinking of the leader, manager, or company that believes people will leave at the drop of a few extra dollars. Think about it: What were *all* the things that needed to happen—the sequence of events, over what period of time—for someone to reach that point? When you really think about it…

People aren't just randomly offered jobs with higher salaries out of the blue (most of the time, anyway). They aren't just walking down the street on their way to get coffee when someone pops up and offers them a job. Even at a networking event, it's rare for someone to walk up to them with an incredible compensation agreement in hand:

- They had to have a reason to start looking first before that ever happened.
- Their ears had to perk up, and they had to pay attention when they overheard someone chatting about an opportunity.
- They had to be willing to stop what they were already very busy doing during the day to call that recruiter back or reply to that email from the ones who reached out.
- They had to decide to listen to their friend, who was talking about how great it is "over there."
- They decided somewhere along the way that they would no longer wear the proverbial company shirt with the same pride they once had.
- They had to open their ears and be willing to listen...

Ultimately, for a person to take any of these steps, they had to be motivated by something. They had to already be feeling a certain way for any of this to even begin. It's unlikely it was just one thing that happened last week; it became a recurring theme for them—something they were missing or how they were feeling: unfulfilled, undervalued, unappreciated, defeated, frustrated, unimportant, not heard, not understood... and so on.

And then, after all that happens...

- They had to update their resume and LinkedIn profile.
- They had to complete online applications.
- They had to get letters of recommendation and references.
- They had to go through an interview process—possibly taking time off work or scheduling interviews after hours, likely more than once.
- They had to schedule lunches, pretend to have doctor and dentist appointments, use their PTO, or go without pay to make it all work.
- They had to dress up and put on their best impression again.
- They had to invest a lot of time, effort, and energy into it.

I've worked with hundreds of people over the past 25 years. Just in the last five years, most of them have come to me for leadership development. A theme I've seen consistently is that nearly everyone I meet feels *they don't have enough time!* They are *so* busy. They don't take time off for doctor's appointments, they find it hard to leave early to attend their kids' activities, they don't have time to work out or eat properly—the list goes on and on. People *do not* have extra time on their hands.

From what I've observed, unless we are in a great deal of pain or discomfort, we generally won't willingly take the time and effort to go through such an arduous process—unless the cost of it all is truly worth it—in the hope that things will be better elsewhere. It takes a great deal of dissatisfaction and unhappiness for a person to reach the point where they are willing to do all that. This tells us that "more money" offers don't just drop into people's laps out of the blue.

Happy, satisfied employees don't engage in any of the above. How can you recognize the happy, satisfied, and loyal team members in your company?

- They willingly and proudly wear the company shirt (both literally and metaphorically) and speak positively about the company, unsolicited.
- Many times, they haven't updated their LinkedIn profile in years.
- They don't respond to calls or emails from recruiters or competitors.
- When friends tell them how great it is elsewhere, they respond by saying how much better it is where they are.
- They recruit their family and friends to work there or buy the company's products.
- They are so busy and happily focused on making what they have work well for them that they don't make time for distractions.

It's a *very* different attitude. They have to feel a certain way for all this to happen. I aim to encourage *those* feelings and actions in my companies.

Think about the times you've decided to make changes in your career path. If you were happy, satisfied, and felt fulfilled and rewarded where you were, you would still be there. If it was incredible, you wouldn't have left. And if you were getting everything you wanted and needed except for money, you would have asked for a raise before going through all that work. And if you didn't ask for a raise, it only proves my point—you didn't feel like you could, should, or would be treated the way you deserved if you did. If you felt it was worthwhile, you would have asked. But you didn't because there was so much more to it, period. That tells you everything you need to know right there.

If you have people who have left you or your company along the way, realize right now that they had to reach a state of unhappiness with you, your company (or both) to have left. (I realize that's a tough pill to swallow—saying it was a money decision takes the responsibility off leadership.) By the time anyone gets to that point, their mind has already been made up. They mentally left a long time ago—back when they answered that first phone call. This only makes it more challenging, if not impossible, to bring them back once they've mentally checked out.

Were they upset that their raise wasn't what they expected? Maybe! But it's more likely they already felt undervalued and unrecognized before that. Perhaps the minimal raise they received was the final straw that sent a loud and clear message.

When people feel valued, recognized, and appreciated, they are not looking for a huge raise to "make up" for it. There is nothing sending them out into the job market again. We all know what it takes to get back out there—it takes work, and most of us won't do that work unless we have a very compelling reason. And it most likely didn't start with money!

Why do people want money? Your initial answer might be like that of many others I have spoken to: "Duh, Michelle, we all know why people want more money!"

But do we? I've managed thousands of people in my career, and in the last three years alone, I've coached over 200 leaders. And guess what? There isn't one answer. There are *many* answers! And I don't mean they all want to buy different things. I'm talking about what money represents for them, and that goes far deeper than just "things." People don't work just for money.

I have always wanted to make a lot of money. I'm not ashamed to say it. Here's my reason: I was very poor growing up. I was on the free lunch program at school (totally embarrassing!); my mom bought powdered milk and mixed it into the regular milk jug so my dad wouldn't know and complain. I came home from school one day to find HUD Foreclosure papers on the front door. My stories could go on and on—but that's another book altogether! Money translated to security on a survival level for me—food, shelter, and sleeping peacefully, ensuring my family's future safety. I never wanted my family to face the same threats I did. I *needed* to succeed for reasons that were deep, emotional, and even painful for me.

For others, money represents status, being seen as valued, fitting in, and meeting the expectations of their family and friends. Others want to leave a legacy for their families. Some value education and want to ensure their children and grandchildren can attend the best schools, universities, and institutions. And some want to create a life filled with memories and experiences for their children and grandchildren that money can make possible. For some, it's so they can give to their church or the charities they love, so they can feel _____. The only reason we want money is so we can feel _____. And usually, while we know we must sacrifice to create what we want in life, we rarely compromise our current happiness and enjoyment to do it. We have limits on what we are willing to do, how much we are willing to tolerate, and how much we are willing to sacrifice to get there. We want to feel like we are getting somewhere and achieving what we care about most. It's all about how we feel.

Japanese philosopher Ichiro Kishimi writes in *The Courage to Be Disliked* that, as humans, the key to happiness is to be a contributor. Contributing to the world brings a sense of fulfillment. When we have the ability to do that, particularly within our careers, we create the potential for happiness.

Here is the Key, the Secret to It All:

If you can feel _____ in your job every day, you will be satisfied, motivated, loyal, fulfilled, and so much more. If your employer or your business is satisfying your core desire and drive toward the thing you most want (because you know it will make you feel _____), you will stay, and you will be motivated to work hard for that.

On the contrary, if I work somewhere that pays me a little bit more (maybe even a lot more), but I still don't feel _____, then how long will I last there? Because it isn't money that gives us the feelings. It is the beliefs that we think we will have if we have more of it. When we are constantly chasing more money to get that feeling, we remain unfulfilled, unhappy, and disappointed, and we continue to think we need more and more to get that happiness.

Instead, the chase is minimized when we find it in other ways within ourselves through the satisfaction we can find from our present situation. This is the opportunity I am showing you. Everything we do as humans, we do for how it makes us feel or how we think it will make us feel.

Simply stated, we want money because we believe it represents or will allow us to have something that will make us feel the way we want to feel. This is the core message of this book. The core desire of humans is to feel the way we want to feel and/or to avoid feeling the way we don't want to feel.

I am suggesting that we often think money is the answer to our emotions when, in fact, it is another source altogether that enables us to feel the way we want to feel or avoid feeling the way we don't want to feel.

If money were truly the solution to our emotional needs, there would be no wealthy individuals who are depressed, struggling with addiction, or engaging in self-destructive behaviors to cope with their misery. (How many of your favorite celebrities have died for these reasons?) In theory, if money could solve these problems, there would *never* be *any* unhappy rich people. Conversely, there would *never* be *any* happy poor people once their basic survival needs—food, water, shelter—were met. But we know that's not true. There is ample evidence around the world that contradicts this idea.

To address the skeptics and those who might be resisting these teachings, I'm not suggesting that money is unimportant. My husband and business partner, who fully supports this concept and book, began as a disbeliever. He would say, "Michelle, are you really trying to say that people won't make decisions about where they work based on how much they're paid? Or that they won't leave if they're offered more money somewhere else? Really? I don't know about that…"

If you are in that camp right now—and I'm guessing there are many of you—this message is for you. Thank you for being here and sticking with me! I suspect that, like my husband, you will become a believer too.

For those who need to hear me say that money is important and necessary for a business to survive and succeed—according to the definitions of banks, investors, Wall Street, etc.—I wholeheartedly agree. "Devaluing" money is not what I am suggesting here. I am a businessperson at my core, and I fully recognize that our capitalist society is based on money being a fundamental pillar of success. To deny this would be delusional, and this book would lose credibility for the valuable points it aims to make.

In business, particularly in a startup, every dollar matters. Budgets are limited, and careful planning is required to determine where to allocate funds, such as which positions to prioritize. A startup that closes 36 homes in its first year does not need to hire a top CFO at the highest market rate, nor would it be fiscally responsible to do so, considering the business and market circumstances. Companies go through different phases where these decisions need to be continually evaluated. A-players may be necessary for certain roles with the appropriate compensation, while in other instances, B- and C-players might suffice, and the focus should be on retaining and motivating them. Sometimes, investing more upfront may be a worthwhile long-term strategy, while at other times, it might be too early for that. At times, a broad set of skill sets that can wear a variety of hats is appropriate. Other times, a laser-focused deep knowledge is the best approach for your new hire. The point is that strategic financial decision-making, evaluating needs and talent, and creatively enhancing compensation packages should always be part of business planning. I will dive deeper into this in later chapters.

I will also admit that, in many ways, life can be easier when you have money. Life isn't easier because of money, though. Life can be hard, challenging, and complicated, with or without it. But having the security and freedoms that money provides does allow for greater ease and flexibility in many aspects. Importantly, however, money also brings additional challenges, responsibilities, and pressures. Honestly, there are days when I fondly remember the simplicity of life before money was involved. Nevertheless, I would rather face the challenges that come with having money than those that come with not having it. But not everyone subscribes to that philosophy, preferring simplicity and freedom from the encumbrances and responsibilities that money brings.

I want to offer you the idea of embracing multiple philosophies at once. Money and its importance to business, people, and survival can and should remain in place—absolutely. In addition to that, our human brains and operating systems are driven by other factors that deserve at least as much, if not more, weight when we consider the decisions we make, the beliefs we hold, and the emotions that drive us each day.

Rather than "devaluing" the importance of money, I am suggesting that we apply equal or *potentially greater value* to the other ways we are motivated. These motivations can and do coexist. I propose that mastering the skill of understanding what truly motivates us holds as much, and likely more, weight. This understanding will allow you, your team, and your company to achieve greater success. Consider this a powerful way to elevate yourself and your organization to new heights.

Even if, by the end of this book, you only give these ideas a little more weight than you currently do, I believe you will see new and different results. Feel free to hold on to your existing beliefs about money and its power. My only request is that you open yourself up to the idea that this new perspective can complement what you already believe and need not replace it. What do you have to lose by considering it? Let me show you a new superpower that is available to you, one that may have just as much power as money, if not far more.

I will expand on all of this throughout the book, but for now, here are three points to ponder to address any internal struggle or resistance you may be experiencing as we get started.

Point 1: "Money," aka coins, printed paper, and digits on your computer screen, cannot make you feel a certain way: good, bad, or indifferent. They are just physical objects (or computer images) that can't serve your happiness or be held responsible for creating your unhappiness. The only way you can feel any way about those things is by deciding what they mean to you or believing what they say about you. This can be different for everyone and anyone. What it means or translates to for you is likely different from what it would mean for 99 other people if 100 people were polled.

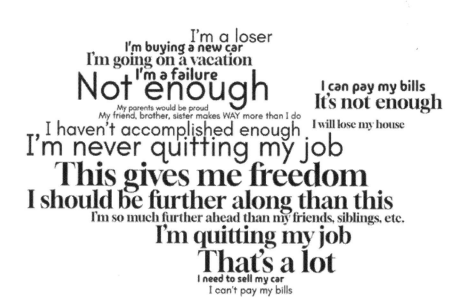

The list goes on and on for what a number can mean for each of us. Each statement generates a different emotion, feeling, or fuel in each of us, proving that it isn't the "$" that creates the feelings—it's the thoughts, beliefs, and emotions about it that do.

Point 2: When all things are equal, what factors are the decision-makers for you? If the money is exactly the same in Company A as it is in Company B, how will you decide which position to take? What other factors are important to you? And most importantly, *why are those* factors important to you? The answer to the *why* likely sheds light on the core of this book: the feeling that you need or wish to satisfy, what you value or prioritize most. Keep this in mind as we continue through the stories and examples ahead.

Point 3: Your earnings and value are a given. What if your earning potential was a given? What if you knew, without a doubt, that regardless of which company you choose, you would always be paid what you deserve, and you never had to question whether that was happening? What if you were already confident in your ability to negotiate the best compensation, and money was no longer a factor in your decision-making? If money were a moot point, how would you choose? What would your decision-making criteria be, then? Similar to the example of those who engage in volunteer or charity work. Their contributions are immensely valuable, and their skill sets are often extraordinary—how do we explain or justify their value as individuals? Your value is a given.

These and other points will be explored further in the chapters ahead. Stay with me. I believe you're starting to see where this can lead, and expanding your thinking beyond what you've been taught and trained to believe all your life might just be a worthwhile exercise.

And by the way, even if—and perhaps especially if—you are an entrepreneur, business owner, or investor, it's still not about the money. You may already be seeing that for yourself.

Let's begin with my story and how it establishes the two necessary structural footings that form The Foundation of success for the Performance Motivator™ System.

CHAPTER 2

How It All Started: My Story

It was August 2007, the beginning of the Great Recession, and I decided to start a home-building company. Theoretically, this was the worst possible time to start any company, especially a home-building company. No matter what industry you were in or what position you held, fear was pervasive. There was no escaping the looming uncertainty and anxiety that were everywhere—not just in the U.S. but globally. The news was grim: the stock market, banks, and gas prices were all in trouble.

In the home-building industry, large corporate builders had stopped or significantly slowed construction on homes already in progress, and their shareholders and banks were not allowing them to start new projects. They were defaulting on land contracts with local developers, some were leaving markets entirely, and many had stopped paying bills to suppliers and trade partners for work that had already been agreed upon or even completed.

Before starting the company, I had been working for one of the nation's largest corporate home-building companies. Despite the market conditions, I felt my position was secure due to the company's needs during those difficult and challenging times. But I was working insanely long hours to stay caught up, covering multiple positions due to a hiring freeze, and doing everything I could to keep our team and division on track. All this with a two-year-old at home. I was missing out on the milestones of being a new mom with a toddler, neglecting basic self-care like sleep, eating well, exercise, and doctor's appointments. So, while I never thought my job was at risk, I was sacrificing everything else in my life each day.

I had been approached by two previous land development partners to help them solve a problem. They had developed some beautiful communities for some of the big corporate builders who were now backing out, leaving these partners burdened with debt and banks demanding payment. While I had dreamed of starting a home building company one day (and they knew it), this wasn't exactly what I had in mind! I expected it to happen later in my career, with more experience under my belt and in a stable economic market. I certainly didn't expect to walk away from my high-paying corporate job and risk it all by not earning a salary with a toddler at home during the global economy's biggest downturn since the Great Depression of the 1930s.

But I made the decision to take the leap anyway. People ask me what steps I took so they can do it, too. My answer is that I don't think there's any way to replicate the exact circumstances and times that shaped my journey. If anyone, including me, tried to replicate it, it would be impossible. We are in very different economic times now; there are more female leaders, financial institutions have changed, and many other factors are no longer the same. In some ways, it might be easier now, while in other ways, there would be new and different challenges. Regardless of the circumstances, though, there are always lessons, takeaways, and fundamental ingredients that are necessary to achieve success, no matter the goal. As I continue sharing these stories, I will reflect on some of the most valuable lessons that I believe can help shape anyone's success in their pursuits.

Your next question might be: Why would you do that?

Why would I leave my secure corporate job to take a risk, live off my savings, with no guarantees of success?

It wasn't an easy decision. It was scary. It was risky, maybe even a bit crazy to anyone watching from a distance. But I knew, in every way, that it was what I needed to do.

These decisions will make more sense as you learn more later in the book about my story and my own Performance Motivator™.

First, I was working over 70 hours each week, including nights and weekends. I was just another number in the big corporate culture at that time, carrying a heavy workload through layoffs and a stressful, demanding environment. Everyone in that environment, including the decision-makers, was just trying to hang on.

I decided that if I was going to work that hard and make such significant sacrifices, I wanted to depend on myself and see what I could achieve with that hard work—for the direct benefit of me and my family. As a 32-year-old woman in a male-dominated industry, this was an opportunity to prove to myself what I was capable of accomplishing.

Lesson learned: I love hard work, and I encourage everyone to work hard for the goals they are passionate about. Hard work and long hours are sometimes necessary; just make sure you're pursuing what you truly want.

Second, I've learned many times that plans are just ideas that give you a target, but you really have no idea how things will play out. Getting stuck on your plans and how you think things *should* happen can limit you from being open to unexpected opportunities. Even though this wasn't the time I had planned or the ideal circumstances, this opportunity was presenting itself right in front of me. Maybe it would be available later, but it was there at that moment. What better time than now to give it my all?

Lesson learned: Don't lose sight of your goals while you're taking steps toward them. It's easy to get caught up in the day-to-day tasks, but we must pay attention to the opportunities that come our way, or we risk missing the very things we're working toward.

I also wanted to set an example for my child—to show what his mom could achieve—which was a driving factor for me. Learning, growing, and taking on new challenges have always been motivators for me, and this was an incredible opportunity to do just that.

Ultimately, I trusted myself to give it my all. If it didn't work out, it wouldn't be because I didn't try my hardest. I was confident that I could find a job if I ever needed one again.

When we started, there were no grand dreams, no big goals, and no aspirations to sell the company one day. It was purely a survival move. That's it. We didn't even have to make a profit. We had one and only one objective: We wanted to purchase the minimum number of lots to appease the banks and avoid foreclosure on the development projects. That was it.

Money was not the company objective. The prevention of the loss of money (and much more) was the only company objective.

We thought this should be easy, but it wasn't. Anyone who was in business during the Great Recession knows that nothing was easy, and it sounds much simpler now than it actually was.

So, on August 18th, 2007, my two development partners and I started a new company. They chose to take a mostly back-seat, inactive role in the company. They kept tabs to make sure everything was okay, but it was mine to run and make decisions as I saw fit. It was exciting and scary. It was frustrating and exhilarating. It was creative and fun, yet also problematic and challenging. It was hard. Having built a strong reputation in the marketplace and being fortunate in friendships and connections, I immediately made my first hire: a good friend on the construction side of the business. He was an A+ player in the marketplace, overqualified for the position with years of experience and volume, and had recently headed up a huge televised "extreme build" project for his previous company—*A+ all the way!* He ran field operations, and with his help and expertise combined with mine, we were off to a great start. He was paid well, but we both knew he could have made more money staying where he was, at least initially. (More on that later.) We had a slightly profitable first year (without paying a salary to myself: I worked for free in exchange for an equity stake in the company—more on that later, too!), and we were officially on the map, making our mark.

Then things turned bad. We adjusted, hoping for a correction. But things quickly worsened. The market tanked even further; banks wouldn't lend money, were closing our accounts, and sales died entirely. We were in very big trouble.

I'm sure if you're reading this and lived through that time, you may have similar stories of the pain and stress it caused. It was truly a difficult period.

I remember sitting at our conference room table one day and just breaking down. I lost it. I remember asking myself, *What's the point of coming into this office tomorrow? What are we doing? Why bother?* That led me to think about what it would be like to tell my good friend that we would need to lay him off and close the doors. Even though that was happening all around us, to our peers, and to other business owners, knowing it was a risk didn't make the idea any easier. He had trusted me to ensure he would have a secure job and paycheck to pay his bills. How could I face him or his wife, one of my very best friends, if the worst happened? And if the worst did happen, then what would I do? How would I pay my mortgage, and could I even sell my home if I needed to? It was absolutely devastating.

No sales and no money meant we couldn't meet our objective of purchasing the minimum lots required to pay the bank debt. And you probably know what comes next—the "F" word: Foreclosure. In the home-building business, that usually means personal bankruptcies as well. Many building companies fell victim to this at the time. Unlike large, publicly traded builders, small private building companies are required to sign personal guarantees with banks to get loans. If those loans cannot be paid, they lose their collateral—their personal homes, the money in their bank accounts, and their other possessions to the banks. Unfortunately, through no fault of their own, many families lost everything they had because of this crash. We saw people we knew and loved, who had built incredible success through hard work over their lifetimes, even over generations, lose everything. It was the scariest financial time I've ever known, and I hope we never have to experience it again. Not only that, I swore never to forget the lessons this time taught me.

The idea of losing everything you've created in your life—your home, your cars, your children's future, everything—is beyond terrifying. Not to mention the difficulty of regaining creditworthiness for many years to come. The emotions of this time were truly frightening.

But some valuable lessons that I will never forget came from it, and for that, I am grateful, as it has allowed me to make wiser investments and business decisions as a result that I get to carry with me for the rest of my life-not to mention share with others as well.

This leads us to the first of the Two Structural Footings of the Performance Motivator™ system. In the next chapter, we'll explore the first footing in detail, focusing on the principles that drive both personal and organizational growth.

CHAPTER 3

Structural Footing #1: Relationships

Your real question for me is not *why*; it's *how* I did that.

When things were really bad, we were close to closing our doors. We were all contemplating what would happen next and how we could earn money to pay our bills. Not only were the main investment partners of the company affected, but so were all the tradespeople and suppliers who depended on the industry—and on us—to sustain their jobs and livelihoods. These were not distant corporate entities or faceless shareholders. These were people who lived in our community. They were the parents of our children's classmates, fellow neighbors at church, at the local neighborhood pool, and at the kids' soccer and football games on evenings and weekends. They were friends and acquaintances we had known and cared about for many years, both in our community and in the industry.

Closing our doors would have put them all one step closer to unemployment—or worse. We were watching it happen all around us. This was not something we took lightly. At times, it was extremely emotional and devastatingly scary. To pretend otherwise would be a gross understatement.

We recognized that a sense of community was essential. Working together to solve the problem gave us a much better chance of success than remaining isolated, hoping that something would change. We decided to bring everyone together. We sat down and had heart-to-heart, fully transparent discussions. We told them how bad it was and how we needed to come together to try to solve the problem, or we would all be out of work. If we couldn't sell homes, we couldn't start building homes—and we all relied on the ability to keep building.

We explored creative ways to tighten our belts and structure payment terms that were manageable for everyone involved. We looked at ways to build differently, using alternative materials where possible. Any idea was worthy of consideration. We laid everything out on the table to see what sense we could make of it all and how we could get through this together. It was serious, yet we all remained level-headed in our approaches and proactive in seeking solutions. We were in the trenches together, and we were committed to finding a way out together.

Although we were far from out of the woods, each month, we managed to climb out of the worst of it, treading water and slowly rebuilding from there. It continued to be a slow struggle, but we did it together, as a community. We all had the same things to lose and gain—the same interests at heart. United, we came out on the other side of what was the worst financial crisis we had ever experienced. It was a careful, slow, and strategic roller coaster that lasted about five years before we could make any real headway. But we survived it. We never had to cut pay or lay off any employees. We paid every single bill for work done, never leaving anybody high and dry. We kept our word with all our partnerships. Success is only truly success when everyone involved wins.

> **Lesson Learned:** One of my greatest lessons learned, repeated more times than I can count, is that community and relationships are the key ingredients to success. There are other important keys to success, but without relationships, you have nothing. Having powerful, solid, and authentic relationships allows all other skills, talents, and abilities to come into play. Hands down. This is a lesson I will *never* forget.

As if that wasn't enough proof that relationships are the key to success, let me tell you what happened next. As we began to achieve what I would call "success"—treading water, staying afloat, and continuing to move forward—the other local developers started to take notice. Not only were we selling homes, but we also had high-quality homes, the latest styles, colors, and design trends that others weren't willing to invest in. We continued to maintain our communities as beautiful places where people wanted to live, unlike neighboring communities with overgrown weeds, unkept or even unfinished clubhouses, and entrance monuments—some gated up with padlocks, especially if the banks were involved. There were community pools that had been started but never finished, and families were frustrated that they were paying for something they were not receiving, through no fault of their own.

We never forgot that we were creating homes for families, and we understood the significance and importance of that. Being an early pioneer of a female-led home-building company not only put us in a unique category, but it also defined and shaped our company culture and impacted the industry in new ways. Our designs, our marketing, our recognition of the power of women in the home-buying process—the most significant and emotional investment anyone will make—all contributed to the heart of the culture we created. We knew what defined us, and we lived up to this standard in every way possible.

In many ways, we were disruptors in an industry that had operated in the same way for decades. All these things made people take notice and put us on the map. Local developers began asking how we could help them rebuild, improve, and climb out of their struggles too. Many of these developers would not have considered working with a small, local builder like us before the recession, preferring to mitigate their risk by choosing larger, more significantly funded building companies—the big guys I mentioned earlier. But now, the big guys were nowhere to be found, and we were their only choice! We built relationships with them. We worked on handshake agreements, and if something didn't work, we came back to the table to figure it out. We had to be creative about funding things that needed funding, and we had to work together to be resourceful in crafting agreements that allowed everyone to get what they needed, or as close as possible. Everything we learned, we applied again here, and it worked again. We all won. Our community won.

The lesson that building relationships and community is crucial to success continued to prove itself, again and again.

Lesson Learned: One of the biggest takeaways here is that our company would never have been created, could not have succeeded or grown, and would never have had the opportunities to achieve everything it did if the Great Recession had not happened.

We wouldn't have needed to start the company. We wouldn't have been invited, or even begged, to enter additional communities, and we wouldn't have stood out from the rest with something unique to offer to either customers or employees. The Great Recession created this window of opportunity for us that wouldn't have existed otherwise. Most importantly, it strengthened the relationships we already had within our community and allowed us to forge new ones that have continued to support us and many others.

For me, the Great Recession was the best gift I could have ever been given.

This isn't some pie-in-the-sky affirmation speech telling you that these challenges will make you stronger—although that is true and part of the message. In fact, I would not be where I am today without the Great Recession to thank for it.

We built our company from zero to an $85 million per year revenue company, building 300 homes annually, and becoming the largest privately held builder in our market. We won numerous awards and gained tremendous recognition for reaching significant milestones. Ultimately, we sold the company to the largest publicly traded homebuilder in the country.

If you ever find yourself or your company in times of struggle, uncertainty, recession, or challenge, remember this story. It was *because* of the Great Recession that I have this story to tell.

Lesson Learned: Challenge yourself to ask how this current struggle, this challenge, or this circumstance can be the best opportunity, the ultimate runway to the future you can create. Ask yourself how it can become the gift you've been waiting for, even if it's disguised as the worst possible thing that could be happening.

No matter what you are facing, you are not a victim of it—unless you decide to be. There is an opportunity available if you choose to find it and create it. Lean on your existing relationships and build new ones. Bring value, offer help, and contribute wherever you can. These practices will pay you back far more than they will cost.

We built strong relationships with everyone around us, including our homeowners, local brokers, and through our charity efforts over the years. Our success is because of all of them.

> **Lesson learned**: Giving of yourselves both physically and financially refuels and repowers your team through the challenges. Contribution of one's self is key, and when it's difficult to do that in your role because you don't see results, or when things become routine and unfulfilling... GIVE.

If you had told me that day, while I was sitting in the conference room feeling defeated, wondering how I was going to pay my bills, "This will only make you stronger," I would have had some choice words for you—that was the last thing I wanted to hear!

But now, looking back, I know that is 100 percent true.

Structural Footing #1 in creating the recipe for success in your business is **Relationships**. With them, you have endless possibilities and opportunities. Without them, you only have yourself. Not many successful companies and businesses have found success in a silo.

CHAPTER 4

Structural Footing #2: Company USP

Plato wrote around 380 BC, "Our need will be the real creator," which over time evolved into the saying, "Necessity is the mother of all invention." Going from near foreclosures and almost closing our doors to selling a tremendously valuable and successful company ten years later was a long marathon of growth, struggle, and overcoming obstacles. Climbing out of the recession was hard enough, and we needed time to catch our breath and regroup afterward. But the challenges continued. As the market improved—as you'll hear later in the story—hiring top talent became nearly impossible. Retaining the people we had, as companies began to hire again, kept us on our toes at all times.

As I mentioned earlier in the MONEY chapter during the business planning discussion, our company experienced a variety of different seasons over the next few years. Smart decision-making around hiring was always at the forefront of our planning. We didn't need all A players, but we needed to attract high-quality people we could count on to do the job well (an A player is how *you* define an A player, after all). In many cases, since we were still in growth and struggle phases, they might need to wear more than one hat. Your entire team is unlikely to ever be made up of only A players. Your B and C players bring value as well. They may develop over time, or they may continue to contribute their best at their current level, which serves both the company and them well, compared to leaving altogether.

However, motivating a tired and, at times, unbalanced workforce as we navigated the new work-life balance trend was a leadership challenge that I had to relearn how to tackle. I had a problem that needed solving, so I went to work on solving it. Once I did, I realized I could use that solution in many other ways—jackpot!

Your Company USP, *or your company's Unique Selling Proposition*, is the heart of Structural Footing #2. The long list of what makes your company unique is what becomes the pulse and heartbeat of your company.

Imagine the potential you have for creating something incredibly unique. Every industry has its leader. There is an icon for every business sector. Sometimes that status is related to the size of the company, but often, it is not. These leaders didn't start out that way; they became leaders because they stood out from the rest.

- Apple reinvented the phone as we all knew it.
- Uber's revolutionary car service (who would have thought?).
- Zappos's commitment to customer experience and care.
- Chick-fil-A reintroducing the chicken sandwich.
- Disney, Netflix, YouTube, Facebook, Amazon and many more.

When I talk to business owners and founders, they often tell me why they are different and what makes them stand out above the rest. I listen to what they share, but usually, it's the same bland, vanilla rhetoric I've heard a hundred times before—quality service, great value, a company of integrity and honesty… Blah Blah Blah. We've all heard it before, and while it's always created with great intentions—dictated by upper management and then flavored by marketing—it's not enough.

Did you know that you needed a phone that did everything else for you as well before it was created? No.

Did you think you needed a different chicken sandwich served to you in an improved way? Probably not.

Did you know that you needed a better experience for your shoe shopping? I'm guessing that's not likely either!

Zappos didn't become who they are by making vague statements like, "Great customer service." They made a decision that it was what would define them and that every decision, person, color, system, process, etc., would revolve around ensuring that commitment would be guaranteed. They would live or die by that commitment. There's a big difference!

Before starting my home-building company, I worked for one of the big national builders (not the same place I started, another of the other big nationals). As you may or may not know, the buying power of any national company in any industry comes from purchasing high-volume quantities of the exact same product, brand, series, etc. This strategy offers cost savings and rebates when working with local warehouses, trades, and installers. The fewer color SKUs (options) they need to stock, the better it is for them. No custom orders or wait times mean they can quickly fulfill orders and get paid, allowing them to offer lower prices to the company and, in turn, lower prices to the consumer. This is a highly successful, well-received business model for high-volume, value-driven companies and consumers, maximizing production speed and cost savings. When used, it proves to be highly effective, as it did for many high-volume home-building companies in the early 2000s. Homebuyers could get upgraded cabinetry, granite countertops, more tile, and upgraded appliances included in their homes for the same price as homes without those features. Win-win for all!

The only downside was that every home looked identical. You would walk into a home and then see three more and not remember the difference between any of them. The same cabinets, same tile floor, same countertops, same carpet color—repeated over and over again across the 300+ homes in any single community with four-floor plan offerings. This model worked fine while the market was booming, despite occasional resistance. There was no incentive for builders to allow for more personalization or changes because the market was hot, people were buying anyway, and buyers accepted the value even if they didn't love the lack of options.

However, once the market began to tank in 2006 and 2007, nobody was buying homes at all. There wasn't much incentive. Builders were slashing prices but still couldn't sell. Most people were content to stay in their current homes and didn't see the value in moving, especially if they couldn't sell their own homes.

When I started our small company in 2007, I started from scratch. We had no pre-designed homes, no negotiated pricing for specific styles or colors—nothing was in place. I had the luxury of starting over. I worked with a local home designer to create up-to-date floor plans and exterior elevation designs that people wanted—new and modern for those buyers. I designed exterior and interior color palettes that were fresh and different, in line with the latest designs. Our first ad campaign was "Looking for something different?" with a picture of a blue strawberry. We had a rule that no home would be vanilla. We were the anti-vanilla new home builder! It was all about the customer's personality, creating something that was "all about them" and what *they* loved.

Our pops of color and new and interesting tile designs put us on the map. And because the market was struggling, we negotiated competitive pricing with our suppliers and trades, allowing us one crucial advantage in this challenging market: *If there was just one family who could buy a home, we would make sure ours was the one they chose. Ours would stand out as the home they fell in love with, the one where they could see their children coming home from school, creating memories—the perfect home for their family. It became an emotional purchase again, as homes always are and always have been—rather than just settling for ugly, dated granite countertops and lacking the perfect homework area for their kids, but at a discount from what it was listed for last month.*

Later, our company tagline changed to "Homes with a Touch," emphasizing that it was all about you, with a woman's touch. The "you" was specifically targeted at women. Interestingly, most home builders were (and still are) men, yet the home-buying decision is mostly made by women. It made perfect sense for a woman to design a home based on what women want and care about most. That's what we did.

This concept shaped the culture of our entire company. We were sought after by developers, trade partners, investors, and, most importantly, by talented individuals who wanted to be part of what we were creating.

Our story is a small one, just a blip on the radar compared to many other large companies that have achieved their Unique Selling Proposition (USP). We put ourselves on the map and became significant and successful because we didn't stay bland; we were anti-vanilla. Had we played it safe, doing the same as everyone else, we would have blended in with the crowd and lost to the big guys all day long, never recognizing the opportunities that we were able to seize in the future.

This process involved hard work—market research, knowing our competition, understanding our audience, and identifying their current pain points and desired results. We understood our consumers and the market, allowing us to position ourselves for success within one of the most challenging selling environments I have ever experienced. Yes, this is important, and most successful companies do it well. But many fall short by stopping there.

The talent pool sought us out. We created a reputation that was woven into the fabric of our entire organization: The homes we designed, the trade partners who were part of it, the employees who delivered, the processes and promises we met, the entire experience and *being* that we created could be seen, heard, and felt. That is what creating a culture entails. That is what the experience of it is like. This means that a negative culture can also be experienced. Culture already exists. It's just a matter of what that experience is for those involved. Leaders can define it, shout it from the rooftops, and write it on the walls, but is it experienced as intended by everyone who is part of it? That is the question to be answered.

Applying the same market research, understanding, and competitive evaluation to define what the company stands for—and allowing it to become the fabric of your entire organization—is what will attract top employees as well. When you truly understand what employees want, how they think, what pain they are in, and what problems they want to solve, you can win against the competition in the talent game too. When you win in the talent game, you win in the market share game. When you win in the market share game, you win in the branding, reputation, and bottom-line success game all day long.

There is a big focus on this area of research, and companies allocate large budgets each year for marketing—both in researching what consumers want and in marketing to them successfully. Yet, we rarely use these insights to attract talent. Sometimes, our talent is attracted to us for the same reasons as our customers, but since we are all motivated by different things, companies miss out on a significant portion of the talent pool by not making an investment in this area. And most importantly, we aren't leveraging what we already do well and using our USPs to attract and motivate talent. The chapters ahead will explore how to use the one thing that makes you unique— your USP—and apply it to meet the different motivations people have.

> **Lesson Learned**: You don't need to have different things for every person. You just need to know how to apply what you already have to appeal to a diverse range of people.

This process led me to do a little research. Statistically speaking, what are employees looking for in a workplace culture? I spent some time looking into it and testing the theories.

Here are the results: The top five attributes when rating a company's culture are:

- Honesty in Communication
- Performance-based metrics
- Accountability and Fairness
- Cooperation and Teamwork
- and most importantly, The Leadership

As you evaluate the culture of your company, take some time to understand how your employees currently rank the company on these criteria. Get feedback, dig into why they see things the way they do, and understand their perspectives. This information will help you shape the culture you want to intentionally create for your company.

When considering leadership, I had to spend some time exploring what makes a great leader. Most of the time, we can recognize them. We notice some of their traits, their style, their personality. But how do you define a leader?

Here is the definition I chose to adopt: *A leader is a person who maximizes the efforts of others through social influence toward a goal or objective.*

I find this to be an interesting definition. It does not specify that the person must hold a particular position within the hierarchy. They may or may not have a big personality or dominant presence. In fact, their styles could vary widely. They are simply people who influence others and find a way to maximize others' efforts. It doesn't mention that they must do it the same way for every person consistently or that there is a right or wrong way of doing it. It also states that they influence toward a goal or objective, but it doesn't specify that the goal must be a "good" one or one that everyone likes or wants.

To further explore the attributes of a great leader, I looked into what employees seek in their leaders. Statistically speaking, employees are looking for leaders who are:

- Approachable
- Accepting
- Connecting
- Authentic
- Courageous, and
- Passionate

Now that you understand this definition and the attributes sought in a successful leader, you might start to see certain individuals as leaders when you would not have regarded them thus before. On the flip side, you may currently have people in positions of authority who do not fully embody this definition and who have the opportunity to develop further within your organization. Whatever position you find yourself and your organization in regarding leadership, the most important takeaway here is that leadership is a substantial factor in establishing the culture of your organization. One could argue that it is the most important factor since all other factors are established, enforced, and modeled by the leadership.

One of my favorite concepts lately is creating "Your Signature Culture." We have the best product, unmatched quality, the best team, and we know we are the best. While this may seem arrogant at first, it's not. We fully expect others to have their successes, attract their people, and run profitable businesses, too. Instead, we simply know who we are; we are confident and secure in our place and what we offer—and equally clear on what we don't offer and who we don't serve. There is pride in our decision-making, our empowerment of people, and our love for what we do, who we do it for, and why we do it.

A client of mine once told me she wanted to create an "Elite Experience" for her client base. When that statement becomes a company mission, it sets an elite tone for everything. This translates into creating an elite team, having elite processes, making elite-level decisions, offering elite-level training, and operating at an elite level in all aspects of the business. It requires everyone on the team to live up to this elite standard. It creates a culture where the team holds each other accountable to this elite status—including the owner and the entire leadership team—because one failure to meet the elite standard lowers the standard for the entire team, calling the elite status into question. It attracts elite clients and repels those who are not. This is *powerful!* It raises the level of the entire company and business model, and the opportunities and doors it opens change dramatically as a result. We don't just want to *say* we create "Elite Experiences"; we decide that every decision we make or don't make, every person we hire or fire, every way we hold ourselves accountable and responsible each day aligns with the decision to fully embody an elite approach. Make "Elite" a clear and distinct brand throughout.

When you create your Signature Culture, your people feel lucky to be a part of it, grateful to work with such a high-quality group where they belong and are valued. They do their best to raise the standard of the entire company. They appreciate it. They love it. And they will bring their very best because of it.

When you create your Signature Culture with your Company USP, everyone must earn their place on the team. This includes new talent coming in, the existing team, and, most importantly, the leadership. Leaders set the tone for whether your Signature Culture's standard is truly upheld across the board. If the leaders are not setting that tone, they have not earned the right to keep their position and rank. Period. So, have the safety nets in place, the accountability checks, and the standards set. If you are serious about your

"Signature Culture," hold everyone accountable to it, including yourself, if you are the one at the top.

As the Founder or CEO, ask yourself:

- Am I living up to the standards and level that I have outlined as our mission in every way?
- Where have I faltered?
- What decisions, choices, or even exceptions have I made that do not align with the standards I have set forth?
- Am I holding myself accountable?
- Am I truly holding others in my immediate charge accountable?
- Have I empowered anyone on my team to hold me accountable?

We want people to work for our company not because we pay the best out there, but because there is something far more incredible available for them—and for us.

Here's what you gain:

- You want to attract and retain your top talent so your business thrives, your turnover is low, and you save money and time. This makes your life easier so you can focus on your real job rather than constantly hiring and training people.
- You can be proactive rather than reactive when someone says they are leaving, so you're not forced to throw more money at the problem to fix it.
- Fewer people seek opportunities outside the company when they are satisfied where they are. This allows you to create more loyal followers, be seen as a high-quality asset to the organization, and maximize your own value—leading to more opportunities and greater satisfaction.
- Higher morale means better quality, improved job satisfaction, higher customer satisfaction ,scores better problem-solving, and

collaboration. The leaders create a smooth-running machine that allows them to rank far above their competition.

I could go on and on about the benefits of creating your Signature Culture with your Company USP, applying my principles from the *It's Never About the Money* concept, including the Performance Motivator ™ System. But the only way for you to know if they work is to give them a try for yourself. Apply them in your own way, with your personality and what is most important to you. Find your company's unique identity and what it stands for. Use that.

Let all this fuel you to create an incredible company and team that achieves success in new and different ways than ever before.

As mentioned earlier, most of life's best inventions and ideas have been created when times are desperate, and you have a problem that must be solved. This was no different.

Imagine leaving your secure job, great benefits, and excellent compensation package at a time when you have a young child, during the biggest financial downturn and crisis known, while banks and stocks are plummeting to start a brand-new home-building company with no salary, living off your savings, and no guarantee of success.

Now, imagine trying to hire people to come work for you and this company during this time. As you can probably guess, most people were not willing to jump ship and take any risks during that time.

There were plenty of people being laid off. It's not as though there wasn't a labor force available. But let's be honest: The top talent, the ones I had been fortunate to have before, had not been laid off. And, of course, they were exactly the talented people, the right players, who I wanted on *my* team. Why not?

But, on top of the issues of attracting them to me, there was an added complication that I couldn't pay salaries at the top levels that the large companies were able to offer. Not to mention, back then, I couldn't even offer health care benefits. There was no universal healthcare, and we couldn't afford a company plan! This added another layer of challenge to my grand idea of starting a brand-new company at the worst possible time and attracting the best people to work for me!

I knew I had to be resourceful and creative. This was crucial. I wanted to set us up for success right from the start, and recruiting A players was a key strategy in accomplishing that. After all, the most important structure of a home is its foundation. Without a solid foundation, the rest of the structure is at risk. People are the foundation. Starting a home-building company with a strong foundation was non-negotiable.

I began drawing from my experience and knowledge from the world of sales training, where we spent extensive time training our sales teams to understand the emotions of buyers during their home-buying journey. Understanding the emotions of buyers—how they make decisions and what truly needs to be satisfied at their core emotional level—was how we served our home buyers best.

I knew that the same principle applied to all humans in any decision-making process. It all begins at an emotional level, not necessarily a logical one. This is the reason someone goes house shopping thinking they want a one-story home but ends up buying a two-story with the primary bedroom upstairs, or why a couple goes to buy a family car but leaves with a new Jeep with the top off or a red two-seater convertible. It all boils down to the same thing: satisfying our emotions. I knew that the decision of where you work and whether you decide to leave or stay is tied to emotional satisfaction.

Emotional satisfaction can only come from one thing: a belief or a decision about what you think something stands for, what it means, how it can make your life better or worse, and how it will help you achieve the result you want so you can feel the way you want to feel.

I had to get creative and consider all the ways in which I had an advantage over the other companies where these A players worked.

Most had not been laid off, but many others around them had. During this season of recession and real estate downturn from 2008 through late 2012, several factors were at play in the market and economy:

1. Consolidation meant wearing more hats.
2. Longer work hours and higher demands.
3. Low morale and concern for what could happen next.
4. Workplace culture decline and lack of personal empathy toward employees.
5. Hiring freezes, salary caps/reductions, and reduced or eliminated bonuses.

These translated to burnout, home life stress, dissatisfaction, fear and worry, health issues, and more. People were unhappy, not treated well, and were concerned about what was next—all while missing time with their families and struggling to keep up with it all. No, they hadn't been laid off, worrying about whether they could pay their mortgage and other bills, but they had plenty of other very real concerns, fears, and worries—constantly aware that they could be next to join their laid-off peers at any moment.

This was the beginning of my recruitment efforts and set the tone for what I needed to do.

If I could solve these problems for them at their core emotional level, I could appeal to some of the best talent in the market. And I knew I could. I had something to offer them that they would value, and perhaps even more importantly, I could be selective about whom I wanted to offer this valuable opportunity. This was both empowering and exciting.

This is not to say that these concepts only work during challenging times. In fact, they are particularly effective during tough times. But if they can work so well during the biggest challenges, it only proves how powerful they can be in any market conditions.

This was the beginning of the patterns, trends, and concepts I created. While it took several years to refine as I learned and gathered more data, these principles became a tried-and-true, proven method for me in recruiting, attracting, and hiring. They helped in retaining and motivating everyone to create a well-rounded team and our Signature Culture of success.

Exercise for you:

Answer these questions and really do the research on them:

1. Who do you want to attract to work for you?
2. Who are your competitors, and why or why don't people like working for them?
3. What are all the ways in which you have an advantage over the other companies where the A players work?
4. What defines your company culture? What are your values, mission, and purpose?
5. What are the issues they are currently dealing with, and what problems would they like to solve most to be worth making a change?

The answers to these questions shape your opportunities. These are your distinct marketing advantages in creating your USP: what makes you stand out above the rest as a company to join?

The following were my answers at that time:

1. Who?

    a. Attract employed and experienced talent from larger companies within the industry who could bring a great deal to the table (aka, wear multiple hats) in a startup company.

2. Why not them?

    a. Large corporates who were now overworking their teams with long hours and many hats due to the layoffs and hiring freezes,

b. low morale

c. no promises of what was to come

d. bleak outlook

e. miserable cultures

f. instability, no security: company divisions shrinking with the risk of consolidations and potential market exits.

3. **Why us?**

a. An exciting start-up that is moving forward rather than backward, where there is a path to a bright future of opportunities,

b. A place where each person brings significant impact and is relied upon for their efforts, which are easily measured and translate to goals being met.

c. A new approach is needed with a new type of leader who wants to make a mark and do things differently, outside of the industry standards.

d. A need for the structure, processes, and systems that someone with a solid foundation can bring.

e. A genuine appreciation for each person's holistic life, the balance it requires, and the realities of balancing family and health while creating success in our career.

4. **Our Company USP: Our values, mission, and USPs were far more extensively defined, but as a high-level bullet list**

a. A risk with us is better than the risk you're already taking.

b. The future has the potential to be so much brighter than what is being painted as possible where you are right now.

c. Life is not very enjoyable now: family, workload, work culture, health, happiness.

d. We are doing it differently, with a new approach, changing the industry, a new leadership approach; it's time for change. No more vanilla homes! NO more vanilla ANYTHING!

5. Issues to be solved

a. Growth, learning, and who you can become are available here, not there.

b. Your efforts generate tremendous impact for something much greater.

c. You are taking a big risk there, and while this also has risk, it's far less than the one you're in now.

d. We are going to stand for something better than what the industry has already seen; it's time for change and you can be a part of it now to spearhead it with us.

e. You can have the balance in life that you have lost recently because that's what we want again, too.

f. Together we will create a family of people who support each other and create something powerful together.

These were our Company USPs in a nutshell. Spending the time to refine yours will be a powerful step toward creating Your Signature Culture going forward.

CHAPTER 5

Where Money Really Matters: The High Cost of Turnover

The latest research at the time of writing this book shows that it costs the average company in excess of $5,000 to attract and hire a new employee, *plus* recruiter fees (which can many times equate to a large percentage of the first-year salary!). This figure only covers the cost of attracting candidates, reviewing resumes, conducting interviews, and getting the new hire set up with their equipment.

Proper onboarding and training statistics indicate that it takes six months just to break even on a new employee. Those first six months involve training, trial and error, utilizing others and resources to get them up to speed—all while you pay them their full salary, benefits, and any other perks they are entitled to. If the average salary for a manager in the U.S. is $115,567, and we add the cost of benefits and perks, we're looking at well over $150,000 per year. Essentially, it's not until the first day of the second half of their first year that you begin to see value from the expense of the new hire. This new hire costs you $5,000 to bring in and $75,000 for the first half of the year— $80,000 in total—not to mention the other immeasurable "costs" to the business and morale if things don't work out.

This is significant and cannot be ignored. Not only is it imperative to hire the right people in the first place, but it is also critical to ensure they are properly onboarded and trained to maximize the return on that investment. These numbers add up quickly if turnover is high. The bottom line is always important, so we need to look at all the metrics that contribute to it and maximize the return on investment (ROI). The bottom line is that it's vital to watch the bottom line.

Losing an employee is money walking out the door, and it means significant hard costs for replacing them. The soft costs and immeasurables are also crucial factors to consider. These include the decline in quality, missed or lost opportunities, delays due to decreased productivity, and the impact on morale when there are personnel losses—all of which can be substantiated, often on a company-specific level.

This is not to say that parting ways with the wrong people or those who aren't a good fit shouldn't be recognized and acted upon quickly when necessary. However, given the expenses involved, the investment in additional resources, training, or development may prove to be a wiser choice in some cases compared to the alternative.

This leads me to my next point: Turnover is okay. Turnover is necessary. Turnover is healthy. Creating your Signature Culture means that as you up-level, your people will too. They may up-level themselves, grow, and develop—sometimes with your help and sometimes on their own. And sometimes, they may not.

If you work for a large corporation or in certain states with more restrictive employment laws, you may already be thinking this, so it's worth addressing: It can be incredibly difficult to fire someone. When I was running my small company, while I always tried to be fair in coaching and developing employees, communicating expectations clearly, and holding people accountable, at the end of the day, if it wasn't working out, it was relatively easy to part ways. These days, in most companies, it's not quite so simple. It takes a large amount of time, documentation, and often, headaches and suffering to terminate an employee. In some cases, depending on the circumstances, companies may choose not to terminate at all because the risk of liability and legal costs is simply not worth it.

Don't get me wrong; I believe employees should have rights, fairness, and protection from wrongful treatment or termination. But in cases where it's not working out, and you've been fair in addressing it, you may find yourself stuck, paying the wrong person while they do not perform the job or meet the expectations necessary to run your company at its best. (A *big* hit to the bottom line!) All of this highlights the importance of hiring the right person for the right reasons from the start. It's interesting that many times, in the name of *"Saving Money,"* it ends up *costing us* much more than it would have had we done it right in the beginning!

The company will grow and change and require different skills, abilities, and levels. Because your Signature Culture is growing and evolving, the company will continue to attract new talent and different skill sets and experience levels, and it has a responsibility to respond and accept those gifts. This doesn't mean that there is anything wrong with those who have "been there since the beginning." It simply means that things change, and people will evolve and change in their own ways as well. Sometimes, it is no longer a match, and the seasons and chapters come to an end. That doesn't mean there is anything wrong with them, or with you, or with your company.

I had a client a few years ago—the business owner and founder at the time. I met with their executive team, and he proudly announced that in their 20 years of business, they had never lost an employee or let anyone go. I was shocked. Yet, it also explained why I was there to meet with them and discuss how their culture was suffering and why they were struggling to find success. Their team was a mix of some original team members along with a new generation of talent and expertise. There were new executives in place who were supposed to be part of the company's succession plan, but they were struggling to manage and lead the team while this mix was not working well together. While everyone on the team brought tremendous value to the organization and contributed to its success, the leadership's unwillingness to embrace turnover as a positive and necessary part of growth was holding them back. They could not make the best decisions for forward growth and the opportunities the company had in front of it.

Once you accept that turnover is healthy and positive for *everyone* involved, people can make the best decisions for themselves, determining where they fit best and what makes the most sense for them at that point in their lives. It's okay to deter those who are not the right fit for what the company has evolved into. Sometimes, maintaining certain traditions and values is necessary and makes sense. Other times, holding on to past ways and priorities only limits where the company can go. Since our time together, the company has seen some retirements and others transition out. As a result, they attracted a new style of leadership that has turned the company around, allowing it to take full advantage of all that was waiting for it!

Over the years, I've heard many philosophies about hiring from clients and business owners. One of my executive clients used to say, "We just need butts in the seats!"—meaning, fill the positions as fast as you can. Another classic is, "Toss them up on the wall and see if they stick," which means the good ones will figure it out, and the bad ones will fall out. I'll admit there may be times when that approach could be appropriate, depending on the circumstances and objectives.

I have worked alongside many peers who are quick to hire and fire, creating a revolving door of employees, knowing it's a numbers game. The more you bring in, the higher the percentage of getting winners—aka A players—while the Ds, Cs, and maybe even Bs get tossed to the side. "Fire them. Fire them. Fire them," was a mantra the leadership team of one such individual knew all too well.

However, this approach is costly. The hiring process—interviewing, onboarding, and training—is very expensive. So, if you do the math, just make sure it's worth it. Maybe the data will support it, but at least get all the facts before making that decision. I would argue that it rarely is and that there is a much better approach in most cases to attract great talent who will stick around and make you far more money in the end. My system and technique will help you accomplish this.

Many believe that large companies have a distinct advantage over smaller ones due to their larger budgets and access to more resources to create success. While that can be true, and there are many examples of it, I've also seen the opposite to be just as true. This book is for leaders who have influence in large organizations as well as small business owners and leaders. There are obstacles to overcome in all scenarios, and no situation is perfect. What I offer are techniques I learned and developed within a large corporation, which I then applied successfully in my small business. No matter what circumstances you find yourself in, these strategies can be powerfully impactful in your world.

Smaller companies can learn these lessons and implement them for immediate impact, seeing significant results. They can usually pivot quickly, with less red tape to navigate, fewer people to gather, and less effort needed to capture buy-in. Smaller companies have the advantage of quick implementation and an ingrained culture of dedication and loyalty, allowing them to see impact and rewards almost immediately. The results they achieve validate their efforts and create momentum to continue, maximizing the rewards of their initiatives.

Larger companies can accomplish the same things, but each leader within the organization needs to be aligned with the same unified direction, value-driven system, and priorities to ensure these lessons are instilled and embedded into the fabric of the company culture. This takes time and a deliberate, concerted effort to implement and execute. It requires prioritization from leadership to create it, develop the processes and systems to support it and establish accountability for the long-term commitment of everyone involved. As you can see, the time to achieve rewards may be longer on a large scale. However, each individual leader who implements these changes can see an impact on their teams and departments immediately—where it matters most anyway!

Big ships take a great deal of effort to change course. The decision to change at all takes time, strategy, and collaboration from many key players. Slowing down is a process rather than a simple act. Turning and navigating must be carefully coordinated, and then picking up speed again on a new track requires considerable time and resources. A small speedboat, on the other hand, can maneuver and pivot quickly and frequently as new information and market conditions dictate necessary adjustments. In the corporate world, I was able to implement culture and change within my own teams, regardless of what was happening around me, while also impacting my peers and those above me. Both approaches have their advantages, but the ability to execute looks very different for each.

As the leader of a small company, I incorporated these lessons into my everyday operating style. I also attracted and developed the leaders around me in the same fashion, insisting that these philosophies be followed and lived daily. A mentor of mine once told me that one of my greatest skills was that I attracted high-quality, smart people. I had never thought about it before, but when they pointed it out, I realized it was true. I just assumed everyone could do the same thing. Why wouldn't they operate in the same way I did to achieve that result?

In my corporate days, at times, I felt I was nothing more than a number and a replaceable body, working myself to the point of burnout, sacrificing family time and personal well-being to save the company money or make it more profitable. I knew that most leaders and companies *do not* operate in the way I believed was right. My value system was different, and my approach brought me success with my people and team everywhere I went. Not every corporation treats people like numbers. But even when they are so large that they have no choice but to do so at the corporate level, the opportunity for change lies with the everyday leaders who are the boots on the ground. So, I took the time to evaluate this as an achievement that needed to be understood and replicated, along with other lessons I had learned.

What I found consistently is that it almost always boils down to something simple. Most things are not that complicated—we just try to make them complicated. Simple is usually the answer.

If you are part of a large corporation reading this, remember that large companies can weather some market challenges and setbacks more easily. A single misstep here and there can be offset by successes elsewhere without significantly impacting overall performance. However, consider this perspective: Just a 5 percent improvement across the board in each division could equate to a substantial bottom-line improvement for the entire company at the national level bottom line.

How many divisions or regions exist in your company? How would a 5 percent improvement in each of them affect your numbers on an annual basis?

None of these lessons are difficult to implement. None of these lessons are challenging to learn or practice. The challenge lies in ensuring diligence, consistency, and commitment to the long-term benefits. But in the end, they are all quite simple.

The other day, I was sharing these concepts with my 19-year-old son. We had some great discussions around these topics. His response at the end was, "Mom, it's all pretty much obvious common sense." I told him he was right. We know what makes sense and sounds obvious, but as adults, that doesn't mean we do it. We know we shouldn't eat unhealthy foods, or overdrink, and that we should go to the gym daily—but that doesn't mean we do these things consistently. We have our habits. We like our habits. Only until we truly look at them and decide that we don't like our results or see how easy it could be to achieve incredible results will we decide to change those old ways and habits. Simple? Yes. Easy? Logically, yes. In practice, it takes some work to chart the new course. But once you've charted that course, it becomes easy. I'm here to help you chart that new course and make it easy.

These lessons do not cost a lot of money. Most of them cost no money at all. There's truly no legitimate argument for not attempting to implement these changes—other than simply not wanting to. There is no other explanation than that. Throughout this book, I will not only explain each lesson but also outline a variety of ways you can implement them, along with resources and tools, depending on the size of your company and the financial resources available to you. They are intended to inspire you to come up with your own ideas and solutions as well. If you have better ways, I not only encourage them, but I'd love to hear all about them, too!

I didn't go to business school, and I have never had any advanced academic leadership education. That said, I have always educated myself in every way possible in the areas where I knew I needed to grow. Reading books, improving my skill sets, and working on my own limiting habits have all been part of my career advancement and life improvement curriculum. If my company would pay for a class or certification, even partially, I made sure to take advantage of it. And even when they didn't, I invested in myself anyway. I have been fortunate to have many incredible role models and teachers along the way who have guided, supported, believed in, and encouraged me when they could. I've also had many terrible role models who taught me what not to do, how not to act, how not to treat people, and how not to lead. This was equally valuable to me. Aside from these influences, my success has come from the trial and error of my own failures and successes. The school of hard knocks, regardless of your level of education, is always going to be powerful.

Let's face it: Our world desperately needs more great leaders, and I am passionate about developing and supporting anyone on that journey in every way I can. Many of the role models we have around us at work, sometimes at home, and leading the world right now are not ideal. They do not represent who we are or who we want to become. It frustrates me and ignites a passionate fire within me as I watch what I see and hear in the world and in business. But we learn by example and create our own practices and habits as a result, and it's easy to fall into these same patterns of poor leadership.

If you are reading this, you already have an appetite for growth and developing yourself in a better way. I don't take that lightly and will provide you with as much value as I possibly can in this book for your benefit and impact. I firmly believe that no matter what your position, you can influence the world, leadership, your team, and company culture, and overall create a more powerful, confident, and peaceful life for yourself by learning these skills.

If you are at the top of the leadership hierarchy and reading this, thank you and bravo. The impact you have is far-reaching, and being a great role model will allow others to adopt these practices and habits, impacting those around them—your power is multiplied, and using it for good in this way has great potential.

If you are in your early career in leadership or just curious about venturing into leadership roles, I'm thrilled that you're here, too. The more people like you I can reach, the more great leaders can be built and developed, growing into future roles that allow you to empower others on a far greater level for many years to come.

I'm in this for the long game. If culture and leadership don't change tomorrow with the wave of a magic wand, I am okay with that, knowing that the long game is worth it, especially when the troops on the ground are carrying the message and are part of the movement!

Now that we have constructed the Two Structural Footings—#1: Relationships and #2: Company USP—in the chapters ahead, I will outline how I created the Performance Motivator™ System, the foundation on which you will build YOUR Signature Culture. The concepts in the next chapter will help you connect everything you've already put into place and apply it to the team and culture you wish to build.

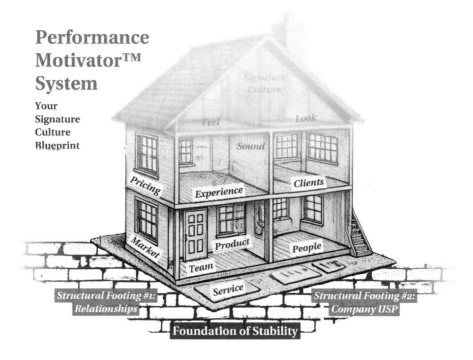

Performance Motivator™ System

Your Signature Culture Blueprint

CHAPTER 6

The Framework and Method: Introducing the Performance Motivator™ System

**PERFORMANCE
MOTIVATOR™
SYSTEM**

While I knew the biggest concerns in the marketplace from a hiring and recruiting effort and standard, it was going to take a next level of emotional buy-in than just those listed in the previous chapter. That was just the beginning. From here, I needed to understand the emotional needs of each of the individuals I wanted to join my team.

Since I hadn't fully developed my concept and categories yet, I was following a more intuitive approach—one I had been teaching for over a decade—to how buyers choose the homes they purchase. I had to start noticing the root of their desires and what they wanted to achieve and feel about their decision.

I quickly realized that this wasn't just a tool for navigating a challenging market or the Great Recession, nor was it limited to competing with the big guys when I couldn't offer top-dollar salaries. This was a way of leading and building a culture that could transform how I attract, hire, motivate, and

61

retain top talent for years to come. Over the course of 10 years, while growing my team to 54 people, I used this process in marketing to new talent, recruiting, conducting deep interviews, and leading my loyal team.

I cannot stress enough the importance of asking the right questions and truly listening to the answers. Taking those answers and peeling back the next layer is key to uncovering what lies beneath. Then, peel back the next layer, and the next, and the next, until you get to the core—the Performance Motivator. If you don't ask great questions, you'll get superficial answers— often the ones they think are the "right" answers. And if you don't listen carefully, you'll miss the one nugget worth tugging on to reveal even more.

There are three keys to becoming great at these skills:

1. Asking high-quality questions.
2. Listening to the answers—both spoken and unspoken.
3. Knowing when to ask for what will lead to the win-win.

This is one of those concepts that, once you learn it, you can never unlearn! You can't put the genie back in the bottle once you've been exposed to this new perspective. It will change how you interview every candidate, how you communicate with your team members, and how you assess a situation when someone says they are leaving. You will see things very differently than you do today.

In other words, you will never operate the same way again—in the best possible way!

❖ Over time, as I listened, listened, and listened...
❖ As I managed, led, and made adjustments...
❖ As I lost great people and not-so-great people...
❖ As I learned, failed, and succeeded...
❖ As I tested, talked, and tested again...

I finally narrowed it all down. I was able to quickly identify the emotional drivers behind why people are attracted to, stay loyal to, and commit to the success of their workplaces. I learned why they choose to start, why they choose to stay, and why they choose to leave.

This was a game-changer—not just for me, but also for the clients I've taught these concepts to and who I've watched apply them successfully. I have distilled decades of work and simplified it for them and for you here.

Now more than ever, people desperately want to be heard, understood, and feel valued and connected. We crave this more than at any other time in history.

Recent shifts in the workplace have created more disconnected cultures, less communication and collaboration, more loneliness and emotional health issues, and lower overall employee satisfaction. This all translates into lower-quality products and services, and, ultimately, lower profits and company value.

The good news is that this is where the opportunity lies!

Neuroscience proves that as humans, we have the gift of feeling emotion, and our emotions drive every action we take, every action we don't take, and every reaction we have to life's circumstances.

Our Performance Motivator™ is the one drive, desire, or emotion that must be satisfied—and all our actions support achieving exactly that.

Introducing the six Performance Motivators: the emotional needs, drives, or desires that direct actions to satisfy a core need, drive, or desire.

The Success Seeker: Focused on the fast track, achievement, learning, and climbing to the top. They know their potential and want to be around leaders who see and help them become that person.

The Impact Player: A trusted advisor who loves being involved in strategy and decision-making to maximize their impact on the company.

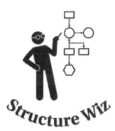

The Structure Wiz: Focused on job security, maximizing benefits, and minimizing risk. Growth and achievement aren't priorities and may even represent unnecessary risk.

The Boundary Balancer: Has a priority outside of work that comes first, and all decisions support that. They may not even need to work but do so for reasons that serve them personally.

The Tribe Thinker: Thrives on team missions and camaraderie. They seek an extended family at work and value the support that comes with it.

The Change Champion: Driven by a bigger purpose, they want to create or stand for meaningful change in the world. This is their primary focus.

Depending on the season of our lives, these drives, desires, and emotions evolve. What drives you at 25 may not be what drives you at 35, 45, or 55. Personally, I evolved into a Success Seeker, driven to accomplish and succeed. However, I've experienced several other Performance Motivator™ phases throughout my career.

Season of Life

The season of life is the key here. Life is an evolving journey. The circumstances of our lives influence the decisions we make. These decisions and thoughts, in turn, fuel our emotions, prompting us to take action to create the results we desire. As circumstances change, so do our decisions, desires, and, consequently, our emotions. This will become evident in the stories you read ahead. Recognizing this is crucial as you continue your leadership journey, especially in terms of the assumptions we make. We may believe that someone we hired years ago is still driven by the same things when, in fact, they may be motivated by entirely different factors today. Personally, I have experienced four different Performance Motivator™ seasons in my life so far. Who knows what the future holds?

There Are No "Best" Performance Motivators

There are no better or worse Performance Motivators. There are no right or wrong ones. Don't get hung up on the names or judge any of them negatively as to which ones might be right for you or others.

- *Example*: Just because you may not be a Success Seeker in this season of your life doesn't mean you don't appreciate success, aren't goal-oriented, or don't want to achieve great things in your life.
- *Example*: Just because you aren't a Tribe Thinker right now doesn't mean you don't value collaboration and work well in a team.

The point is to take the time to investigate and be curious about the truth beneath the surface to determine which one is right for you right now, in this season of your life. This will always reveal itself through your decisions and actions, and even the actions you don't take. There is no hiding from the truth of them. Knowing the truth is powerful. Then you can make decisions with greater empowerment and clarity.

Market Rate Compensation

Paying fairly is still important. I want to be clear that I am not suggesting people should not be paid well for the work they do. Nothing can kill loyalty and dedication more than discovering that you are being paid far below market value while being trusting and loyal to your employer. It is still the responsibility of leadership to be aware of market conditions and changes and to make educated, conscious decisions about compensation packages that are fair, legal, and within the guidelines required by state and local laws and regulations where the company operates. That said, there are many non-monetary forms of compensation. There are ways to structure compensation packages creatively to fulfill both the needs of the company and the potential employee. There are many instances where a few extra dollars are not the answer to satisfying even market compensation numbers. Instead, other structures and perks can make up for it. In some cases, being paid less money in exchange for opportunities to learn and grow or for unique mentorships is far more valuable and a worthwhile trade-off.

Not a Personality Test!

I am a huge fan of personality tests, strengths assessments, and anything that provides more insight into ourselves and others. They are wonderful tools! However, Performance Motivator ™ types are *not* the same as personality tests or other strengths-profiling systems. Personality tests are based on how we've been wired by nature, while Performance MotivatorTM types are purely based on emotions—emotions that stem from thoughts and decisions made individually, influenced by life circumstances. This is why they can and often do change, as they are optional and specific to each person's unique circumstances. Personality tests and profiling systems rarely change or only fluctuate slightly, typically speaking. Performance MotivatorTM types are another layer to consider, another data point, one that hasn't been considered in the traditional leadership sense until now. Paired with other assessments, they provide new perspectives and insights into how a person is motivated today in their life.

Generational, Gender, and Other Stereotypes

There has always been talk about generational differences—their work ethic, what they value, and how they think and operate. It's common to categorize each generation, gender, or other group to notice trends and then try to lead and manage them according to those trends. We all have stereotypical judgments that we have either heard, experienced, or believe: "Those Millennials," "The Gen Z'ers," "The Boomers," and "Gen-X." You probably have something specific in mind when you hear these labels, especially in relation to work ethic, career attitudes, or skills in the workplace.

Stereotypes, Generational differences, and age differences can be taken off the table with this philosophy, making it much easier to develop a real plan that brings results. Generalizing people based on their generation never resonated with me. Yes, I understand that it's easier to generalize or create a stereotypical understanding of what makes a generation tick, what they value, and what motivates them. Science certainly supports these generalizations for broader marketing and demographic purposes. I can see how they can provide some value in certain aspects of decision-making. However, on an individual level, I found that these generalizations rarely applied or, at minimum, didn't serve me much in terms of how to best incorporate people into the team successfully. The Performance Motivator™ System proved to be a far more valuable process, as they were more empowering and created the results I wanted. They allowed me to be in control of my own solutions rather than feeling confined to standards that were nothing more than generalities.

This applies to gender as well. In many ways, generalizing or stereotyping based on gender can also be set aside with these philosophies. In all my research, I found no trend or bias to create a generality or stereotype regarding the six Performance MotivatorTM types based on gender. I found it far more effective to use this concept to manage and lead someone rather than relying on stereotypes or generalizations that are often the default.

The One and Only!

You may recognize yourself in several of these descriptions, and that's okay and to be expected. But at the end of the day, you have one primary motivator right now in this season of your life. You might have some remnants of the past that sound familiar to you. You may have ideas and dreams for your future that resonate with some of these as well. But again, there is only one driving you today, based on your current circumstances, thoughts, and beliefs.

Knowing that there are six different Performance Motivators in existence, roughly 17 percent of the talent available will be in each category, mathematically speaking. *You're probably only speaking to 17 percent of the talent out there right now!* It's normal and instinctual to relate to and communicate with others in the way we think, the way we understand and how we prefer to communicate with ourselves. Yet, assuming that others are motivated the same way we are (our individual 17 percent category) translates to missing the other 83 percent of available talent in the other five categories. What percentage are you currently attracting, relating to, motivating, and retaining right now? Don't miss out on the other incredible humans who have much to offer, assuming others will be motivated the same way you are.

In summary, an individual's Performance Motivator™ is the single need, drive, or desire that dictates their decision-making and actions to satisfy it. It is the #1, non-negotiable, hard-line priority. If nothing else happens, this *must* happen. It is the *one* thing that stands in the way and, therefore, dictates the decision. Here are the highlights:

- **Season of Life.** We are ever-changing, and just because you had one Performance Motivator™ in the past doesn't mean you won't have a different one later in life, again and again.

- **No Right or Wrong Motivator.** Don't judge them. Each one has value and is important.

- **No Stereotypes.** They do not conform to stereotypes based on generations, gender, or anything else. They stand on their own.

- **Not the Same as Personality Tests or Strength Assessments.** While they can complement these tools, Performance Motivator™ types are different as they can change frequently based on life circumstances.

- **Relating to Others.** Your Performance Motivator™ represents *only 17 percent* of the talent population. Learn how to relate to and communicate with the other 83 percent to avoid alienating them.

- **One and Only One.** Even if you relate to other motivators, there is still only *one* primary motivator for you at this moment.

- **Market Compensation is Still Important.** Underpaying someone compared to the market rate can ruin relationships and morale. However, being creative with *compensation* and perks when necessary is key to applying these lessons effectively.

Now that we've defined what a Performance Motivator™ is and covered the key points that support it, let's explore some incredible examples of each Performance Motivator™ in the chapters ahead. In the following chapter, we'll look at the Success Seeker.

CHAPTER 7

The Success Seeker

Success Seeker

From the wide-eyed age of 12, I can remember being a die-hard seeker of success. Raised in a family that chased dreams, my parents constantly told me, "You can do anything," and I took it to heart. I pursued my passions with a hunger to achieve, learn, and grow.

Family game nights were always competitive in our house. Monopoly, with its virtual real estate empire to conquer, was my chance to claim victory-it was my favorite game. Maybe that's what led to my future career and success in real estate! In every role I took on, I challenged myself to achieve and to be in charge. While money sometimes accompanies success, it was never my emotional driver. As a Success Seeker, my motto was, "The sky's the limit!"

At the eager and fairly naïve age of 25, my ambitions were realized when I was handed the reins of a team of 17 individuals, many twice my age. My humbling path as a leader had begun. The drive to succeed, lead, and teach became my purpose. The essence of a *Success Seeker* was etched deep within me as I climbed the corporate ladder, creating success around me. By age 32, when the opportunity arose to pursue a long-time dream of starting a home-building company, I remained focused on making that vision a reality despite the odds being stacked against its success. Tackling challenges and staying willing to do whatever it took led to the company's success.

When I was approached by two development partners to start a new company, I was already working for a stable corporation with a strong compensation plan. So, what lured me? Why did I pay attention when they pursued me? As a Success Seeker, I knew I was capable of creating something so much more, something so much better. In many ways, I believed I could do it better than they could. That may have been arrogant or even naïve, but I believed it was true. I thought I was one of the best leaders in the company, better than most.

If anyone at that time had taken the time to sit down with me and paint a path for what my talents could bring to the company long-term, I would have listened. If someone had recognized that having me as a long-term leader within the company would allow me the opportunity to become the person I knew I could be, I might have pursued that possibility. Instead, two other people *were* paying attention, and they *did say* the things I wanted to hear and that I knew were true. So, I left to pursue my own path. I created a company that was later purchased by the top competitor in the market of the company I had left. Who knows what might have happened or what could have been different? It's not a criticism of them—they had far larger issues and concerns at that time. But the point is valid: Being aware of your people, who they are, and what motivates them is crucial. I was a Success Seeker looking for my path, and I was going to find it NO MATTER WHAT. Money was an unknown risk and an unimportant factor in the decision-making process.

✳✳✳

Here's a fun and ironic side note for you… the company we ultimately sold our home building business to was none other than the very first company where I ever worked and learned everything I knew about the home building industry. Yes, I started when I was 24 years old there, created an incredible career, and then sold them the company I built when I was 44 years old! I gained tremendous mentors, friends, and peers there. Yes, this is the perfect example of Structural Footing #1 coming into play— RELATIONSHIPS!!!

***

Many times, Success Seekers find themselves in various career paths and industries in their pursuit of success. I've worked with and alongside countless high-achieving Success Seekers who have found success in a variety of industries.

As a Success Seeker:

You know who you are and who you can become, and you choose places to work and leaders around you who see and support that vision. Your energy and drive are seen and valued within the organization, and your desire to learn and grow is appreciated by those around you.

You likely bring a great deal to the table whenever you are called upon and intentionally place yourself in positions where you can contribute your abilities whenever possible.

Learning from others and allowing others to teach and guide you is one of your admirable qualities, and your willingness to make yourself available and work hard has brought you great success thus far in your life and career path.

You are goal-oriented and driven toward crossing finish lines, qualities highly desired by most employers and ingredients for great success in anything you do. This means that when all things are equal, you will always lean toward choosing the place that fulfills this Performance Motivator™ for you.

This also means that when this Performance Motivator™ is met, you are loyal and unlikely to be lured away easily (even when things start to become less ideal or just different). When it comes down to it, if Company B offers you a little more money but doesn't show you a path toward advancement, learning, development, or growth, you won't choose it over Company A, which is fulfilling what you care about most, even if it cannot pay quite as much. Your *why* for getting up each morning is to learn, grow, advance, and develop—not for a few extra bucks in the short term.

Success Seeker Words of Caution

As with any blessing in life, it can also be a curse. While this drive has led to your success in many ways, it can also limit your growth and progress. As the seasons of your life change and your priorities shift, old habits can get in the way of creating what you want next.

It's easy to fall back into habits that have always worked, even though they may not serve you toward your next level of goals. Being very clear about your priorities in each season of your life is critical in your decision-making, as you now understand that your Performance Motivator™ will play a significant role in this process.

Success Seekers often struggle with creating life balance and prioritizing their focus. Their emotional driver is the success they seek, often at the cost of other things in their lives that they also value and have a strong desire to achieve. Being aware of this tendency is crucial for you as a Success Seeker as you make decisions, establish priorities, and hold yourself accountable to the boundaries you create. This awareness will also help you recognize when others on your teams, your peers, and possibly even your bosses may be falling into this trap as well. Supporting others in staying focused on all their priorities will be a worthy investment. The costs of health issues, relationship strains, and other stresses typically do not serve the company in the long term either. Unfortunately, this is something I experienced early in my career, and have since helped many others work through their leadership development.

Your desire and need for advancement and growth may sometimes cloud your judgment as you make decisions throughout the day. Sometimes, advancement and growth may not be readily visible to you or even a possibility at all, and it will be up to you to recognize that this doesn't reflect negatively on you—or them. You will need to decide whether to create growth opportunities for yourself within your current circumstances rather than depend on others to create them for you.

Be cautious about making emotional decisions that don't align with your long-term goals. For example, becoming frustrated, disappointed, or angry over not getting the promotion or advancement opportunity you had hoped for might lead you to act in ways that don't serve your best interests—whether in how you interact with others, how you show up, or even in making hasty decisions to quit or change jobs.

These decisions might not come from your best place or fuel, and you could end up regretting them later. These red flags are there for a reason and serve as a reminder to pay attention and ask questions, but ultimately, it is up to you to act from a place of wisdom before making a move. This is how you will make decisions that you are truly proud of, as they will be aligned with what's most important to you.

How often have you heard of scenarios where a recruiter, hiring manager, or leader has made promises and painted a big-picture fantasy for new hires, only to change, delay, or procrastinate on those promises later? When your sole focus as a Success Seeker is on the promises and paths that have been created, it can be easy to fall into the trap of hearing only what you want to hear. This can blind you from seeing the full picture, asking the right questions, and noticing the red flags that are likely very apparent. Being aware of what motivates you allows you to fully evaluate and carefully determine what is best for your future path.

As a leader, it is essential to understand that while you know what motivates you, it will not always apply to others. Assuming that others are motivated the same way you are can cause disconnection with your peers and direct reports. It's important to recognize that Success Seekers make up just one of the six Performance Motivators, which means you are part of only 17 percent of the whole population.

Attempting to recruit, manage, and motivate others your way will limit your ability to connect with the other 83 percent of people. Most of us relate to and speak to others in the way we want to be treated and spoken to. This is human nature. But this is an opportunity for you to understand others better, learn about them, and discover how they are motivated differently.

Success Seeker Needs:

- Opportunities to learn and develop existing and new skill sets.
- A clear path outlining what it takes to reach the next step—whatever that may be.
- Communication and redirection when necessary. Keep the momentum, encourage the drive and energy, and just point them in the right direction.
- Recognition of their wins, achievements, and contributions.
- Rewards: these can often come in the form of additional opportunities to learn, grow, or even train and lead when possible.
- Exposure to the bigger picture when appropriate for the individual and for the business.

CHAPTER 8

The Tribe Thinker

Michelle the Tribe Thinker's Story

Later in my career, I recognized the immense value of creating an extended family within my organization. The people I hired, those under my leadership, became individuals I wanted to care for and whose long-term success I wanted to ensure. I was determined to build a culture where our bond would be the glue that carried us through the challenging and difficult times ahead. This desire to create a family-like culture was partly personal—to fulfill my own need for connection—but it was also for the company to stand out from the rest. I wanted to offer a place where people had names, families, real lives, and felt seen and heard, as opposed to the corporate cultures of the time, where everyone was just a number, replaceable at the drop of a hat. I had come from such a corporate culture, and many of those on my team had as well. I knew I wanted to create something unique and far superior to that. I wanted to create a special company that cared.

As I evolved into a *Tribe Thinker* and began building a company that felt like a small tribe, I attracted others who also valued the tribe mentality. Once I had more Tribe Thinkers on the team, they, as Tribe Thinkers often do, began attracting their friends who shared the same mindset. In many ways, this became an unintentional recruiting tool used by others within the company. The energy and culture that the Tribe Thinkers projected to the world also attracted more business and customers to our company. Homebuyers, Realtor partners, and trade partners were all drawn to this unique and special culture that was being advertised and showcased in ways that no other company in our market had done. None of this could have been planned if I had tried! I can't take full credit for what happened; it all started because I unknowingly initiated it, and it continued because those who loved it also loved to talk about it and proudly share it.

Bob the Project Manager's Story

Bob joined us as an enthusiastic project manager. He was young and not as experienced as the seasoned veterans on our team, but I always love having young, energetic individuals who are eager to learn and grow.

Our team embraced him—teaching, mentoring, and supporting him. This camaraderie fueled his desire for the next step of promotion, along with all the rewards and stature that come with it, but we knew he wasn't quite ready for that leap. He still had a lot to learn.

Sure enough, one day, his manager came in to let us know that Bob was leaving us. We were a bit shocked to hear that he had been offered the big promotion and title he wanted so badly by a competitor in the market.

We faced a tough decision—one you may have encountered too. Should we counteroffer to keep him with the title and more money?

Deep down, we all agreed that promoting Bob prematurely was not in his best interests or ours.

After a farewell gathering and some sad goodbyes, we sent him off with our best wishes. But the story doesn't end there. Six months later, Bob was back, and he was miserable! He quickly realized that it was the team support and camaraderie he valued most. He felt he had been "left on an island on his own" at the new job. Much to our surprise, we learned that day that Bob was not a Success Seeker after all but a Tribe Thinker! He loved working toward a team-driven mission and valued the support of his teammates around him, who felt like an extended family—both inside and outside of work.

Reinstated to the team and now lovingly referred to as Boomerang Bob, he is working better than ever. He's also taken on the role of volunteer Social Fun Director.

I learned that day that, as leaders, it's sometimes our job to help the Boomerang Bobs on our teams see that their Performance Motivator™ is being met right where they are. For Boomerang Bob and Tribe Thinkers like him, it's all about the tribe—it was never about the money.

Had I fully understood then what I know now, I realize that we might have been able to prevent Bob from leaving in the first place. We had many coaching and development discussions with him, but we spoke in our language, not his. We focused on what he was telling us, but we weren't paying attention to what was really happening. Continually discussing his advancement was not what he really needed to hear, even though that's what he was saying. He needed to be shown how much the tribe valued him and that his best opportunity for future advancements would come from what we offered. We knew our culture and team were rare and unique, but unless we communicated that to the employee and showed them, they wouldn't realize how special and valuable it really is for them. Sometimes conversations are enough, and sometimes they need to experience and see it for themselves— but we can at least try.

Jerry the Sales Agent's Story

Jerry joined our team as a Sales Representative during a period of growth and expansion for our sales team. The timing was perfect to add Jerry. He was tall, charismatic, and his energy and personality were magnetic to everyone—not just on our sales team, but with the entire company. He went out of his way, right from the start, to build relationships with every team member. He genuinely liked everyone and always took the time to talk with them, even if just to pop into someone's office with a smile, say hello, and ask how they were doing. He consistently made an effort to be inclusive of everyone. If there were plans being made after work for anything, Jerry invited others to join with his kind and welcoming spirit.

We learned that Jerry had created something similar where he worked previously. That company experienced a significant upper management change, and the leadership and management shifted. The culture changed, and "Jerry's family" changed too, leading him to look elsewhere and ultimately join our small but growing company. Jerry was also a fantastic social media "advertiser" for everything he did in his life. He was constantly bragging about the company, singing the praises of the great people he worked with, and sharing the amazing things we were doing. He was well-networked and built great relationships outside of the company as well. When it came time for our growth to continue, and we needed to recruit more great people to our team, guess who was on the job? Jerry attracted at least four other incredible friends in the industry to join our team. We sold more homes because of him, and we continued to build our great culture and reputation in the industry because of the tribe that was created. While it may have begun with hiring people who would attract more Tribe Thinkers, it continued to draw others to our team—both Tribe Thinkers and those with other motivations.

Jerry is just one more example of how Tribe Thinkers can be invaluable assets to an organization in many ways.

Patricia the CFO's Story

Patricia joined our team as a Controller and quickly rose through the ranks to become the CFO. When she first joined the company, she was a solid Success Seeker—driven, smart, and always looking for ways to learn and climb. Over time, she formed strong friendships with others on the team, and some of her closest relationships were established during this phase of her career. At one point, Patricia went through a challenging divorce, and work became her outlet. She became even more dedicated, working long hours and pushing herself through this difficult time. Her friendships at work helped her through it all. Her extended family lived many states away, and she had no interest or plans to move back home after her divorce.

In one of our conversations, she told me that the extended work family she had created within the company was a game-changer for her. Her desire to climb, succeed, and push for more was no longer her primary drive. Success for her now meant being part of an extended work family within the tribe she had created in her role at the company. There was no opportunity outside the company that she could imagine would cause her to even consider leaving. She genuinely loves and cares for those in her work tribe.

The circumstances of her life had changed, and what she valued most—her emotional driver—had changed too.

As a Tribe Thinker:

Your work life and personal life often intertwine in many respects. Choosing where you work is akin to choosing your friends, your extended family, and your social world. Working with people you enjoy is a significant driver for you, and because of that, you work hard to maintain this dynamic for yourself and to attract and create that culture for others. Others appreciate you for fostering this culture of belonging and acceptance, and it permeates throughout the organization. You are motivated by a sense of belonging, and you are driven to ensure others feel they belong as well. Performing in a way that risks this culture is something you strive to avoid. You provide a critical element that many companies seek to create and deeply value when they have it. This means that other things being equal, you will always choose the place that fulfills this Performance Motivator™ for you. This likely also means that when this motivator is met, you are loyal and, therefore, unlikely to be lured away easily, even when circumstances become less favorable or change. If Company B offers you slightly more money but lacks the sense of belonging and culture that Company A provides, you are not likely to make the switch. Your *why* is far bigger than money, and you wouldn't trade an accepting and welcoming family-style culture for a few extra dollars at the end of the day.

Words of Caution

As with any blessing, this can also become a challenge. While this approach has served you well in many ways, it can also limit your growth and progress. As the seasons of your life change and your priorities shift, these habits can hinder you from creating what you want next. It's easy to fall into the habits that have always worked, even though they may no longer be serving your current goals. Being very clear about your priorities in each season of your life is critical in your decision-making, as you now understand that you have a Performance Motivator™ that will influence it. There will be times when shifts and changes cause company cultures to evolve. Directions and perspectives may change. There will be times when the welcoming and accepting culture you value may be questioned or redirected by leaders with a different strategy for achieving the business plan. You will need to recognize that this doesn't mean anything about you—or them. You will need to decide whether to be open-minded and consider the new perspectives or allow these changes to drive you toward making emotional decisions that don't align with your true goals.

In other words, becoming frustrated, disappointed, or angry over a change in direction or a decision that differs from past priorities might lead you to operate in ways that don't serve you—how you interact with others, how you show up, or even making decisions to quit or change jobs as a result. None of these decisions would have been made from your best self or with your best energy, which usually means you might regret them later. These signs are there for a reason. They prompt you to pay attention and ask questions, but it is up to you to operate from a place of wisdom (recognizing that your happiness and fulfillment are not dependent on people or things outside of you) before taking action. This is how you will make decisions that you will truly be proud of, as they will be aligned with what's most important to you.

As a Tribe Thinker leader, you will need the support of mentors and your team to keep you in check when your decision-making is driven by the love of the tribe. You may see your team as part of your family, which can make business decisions challenging. Being clear about the lines between the tribe's culture and running a smart and profitable business will be essential for maintaining clarity. Tribe Thinkers often struggle with having difficult conversations, holding their people accountable, and making the decision to terminate employees when necessary. I have seen leaders struggle with this far too often, sacrificing performance for caring for the tribe member.

Tribe Thinker leaders will benefit from recognizing that not everyone wants to participate in all tribe activities all the time, and that's okay. If someone is motivated by a different Performance Motivator™, they may potentially view the tribe activities as a distraction from their goals and not aligned with their Performance Motivator™. Don't let your Tribe Thinker motivation work against you and inadvertently create the opposite result with your team.

What Tribe Thinkers Need:

- Team-driven missions.
- A sense of belonging within the company.
- Collaboration and projects that encourage joint efforts and contributions.
- Support through challenges from those around them.
- Social connections and an extended work life that blends into their personal life.
- Opportunities to enhance and bring value through their social influence and abilities.
- Guidance in decision-making that is motivated by their love of the tribe.
- Development to remember that not everyone shares their motivation.
- To boost camaraderie and morale but require clear boundaries for tough people-related decisions.
- The ability to support both the group and individuals through loss.
- If you have a Tribe Thinker leader on your team, it will be important to provide them with development opportunities to remember that not everyone is motivated the same as them.
- They bring a tremendous amount of camaraderie and morale to the culture but will need clear boundaries when it comes to more challenging, people-related decision-making.
- Managing Tribe Thinkers can be challenging when a key member of the tribe leaves. Being able to manage the tribe as a whole, as well as the individuals within the tribe during times of loss, is a key skill to develop.

CHAPTER 9

The Boundary Balancer

Bonnie the Warranty Manager's Story

Hold on tight as I introduce you to Bonnie, our legendary warranty manager. She single-handedly manages the roller coaster of emotions tied to people's homes with grace and ease. Her patience and empathy are truly gifts that our entire team loves and appreciates! We often refer to her as a saint, and I think you might agree!

But there's more to Saint Bonnie than meets the eye. She's also a single mom, having lost her husband several years ago. She shoulders all the responsibilities that come with parenting with purpose and love. Like clockwork, she leaves the office each day at 3 p.m., her heart set on picking up her little one from carpool. Together, they return to the office, where her sweet daughter, Abby, does her homework at the table next to her while Bonnie completes the day's tasks.

As a *Boundary Balancer,* Bonnie's primary emotional motivator is her daughter, yet her commitment to her job, the homeowners she loves, and her team never wavers. She knows that balance is key, and because of that, she is a powerhouse of productivity, accomplishing more in her 30-hour week than some people do in 40+ hours.

If we were unwilling or unable to accommodate her needs, she wouldn't hesitate for a second to find something elsewhere—even if she lost the 401(k) match, or the company-paid gym membership. You see, Bonnie doesn't *need* to work at all. She chooses to for many reasons, including the peer socialization that she appreciates (it could be easy to mistake her for a Tribe Thinker here), having a sense of purpose, and, most importantly, being the best role model she can be for her daughter. As a Boundary Balancer, accommodating the priorities and demands of her holistic life is the most important thing for her, and *it's never about the money.*

Anna the Attorney's Story

Anna is a successful attorney in her law partnership. As she built her practice and achieved success, she was also creating a successful family life at home. She had two kids—a curly-haired three-year-old daughter named Sage and an 18-month-old son named Jake—when she found out she was pregnant with baby number three. She had worked hard to balance it all thus far—the demanding workload of her clients and practice, as well as the demands and pleasures of her husband and children. She enlisted the help of a nanny and others without hesitation along the way to make it all work. But having baby number three on the way gave her a new perspective. This change required her to rethink her priorities and determine what made the most sense going forward.

Walking away from the practice she built over ten years was not an option for her. So she had to make some tough decisions and put some serious boundaries into place.

By the time Anna had Rose (baby #3), she had arranged to work only 2.5 days per week after returning from maternity leave. She made arrangements with the other partners to manage her workload adequately, hired an additional paralegal for her team, and was deliberate in choosing her clients and cases, managing it all within the guidelines she had established. While challenging, she knew that the only way it was going to work was if she stayed the course and was strict about cases, hours, clients, and, most importantly, delegating. She knew that she had to entrust others to take on tasks that were not a top priority at work, just as she did at home. The sacrifices were worth the rewards. It took cooperation from her partners as well. Fortunately, it was seen as a win-win for both sides, and they all worked hard to make it work.

As a Boundary Balancer

You enjoy working and bringing value and impact to a place where it is appreciated and needed. You likely also enjoy being surrounded by people and environments that add richness to your life. You are fulfilled with the responsibilities of a job with a good company. You also know that in this season of your life, even though your job is very important to you, it is not your top priority. Due to either circumstances or choice, the responsibilities you have outside of work are far greater than the ones you have at work. This necessity for balance is critical to you. When a company has someone like you, they are likely to be appreciative of what you bring to the table and are very happy to accommodate your personal needs outside of work. The benefits you bring far outweigh the accommodations that need to be made to have you on the team. It's a win-win for all.

This means that when all things are equal, you will always lean toward choosing the place that fulfills this Performance Motivator™ for you. This also likely means that when you have this Performance Motivator™ met, you are loyal and, therefore, unlikely to be lured away easily (even when things start to become less equal or just different). When it comes down to it, if Company

A will pay you a little bit more but is unwilling to accommodate your personal priority needs outside of work, it's not going to be the choice you make—when Company B is fulfilling what you care about most but possibly cannot pay quite as much. Your *why* is far bigger than money, and it's a deal-breaker for you: No further discussion is needed—you cannot be convinced otherwise.

Boundary Balancer Words of Caution

As with any blessing in life, it can also be a curse. While this has proven successful for you in many ways, it can also limit your growth and progress. As the seasons of your life and your priorities change, these habits can get in the way of creating what you want next. It's easy to fall into the habits that have always worked, even though they may not be the ones that really serve you in reaching your next level of goals. Being very clear about your priorities in each season of your life is critical to your decision-making as you now understand that you have a Performance Motivator™ that will influence your actions. It may be challenging for you to navigate at times. Guilt may play a role in the decisions you make. Depending on your background, position, and expertise, it may be challenging for you to honor the decisions and priorities you are making, knowing what you are giving up on the professional side.

In previous seasons of life, you may identify and have the remnants of being a Tribe Thinker, an Impact Player, a Success Seeker, or any of the other PMs. This will be a struggle in your mind, so be certain that you are clear about your priorities and stay true to them. Either way, your true Performance Motivator™ will be the winner no matter how much you struggle, argue with it, or even deny it at times.

Additionally, business needs and plans change. When they do, leaders may need to make different decisions about what they need and how they need to go about achieving their business plans. That may not include you being a part of that, but none of us really has any guarantees anyway. It will be up to you to recognize that it doesn't mean anything about you—or them.

You will need to decide whether to view it with the facts in mind, or to allow it to drive you toward making emotional decisions that don't lead you down the path you really want to follow. In other words, becoming frustrated, disappointed, or angry over a change in direction or a decision that is different from what has been allowed in the past might lead you to act in ways that don't serve you—from how you interact with others, how you show up, or even making decisions to quit or change jobs as a result.

None of these decisions would be made from your best place or with your best fuel—which usually means you could regret them later. These flags are there for a reason and serve as signals for you to pay attention and ask questions... but then it is up to you to operate from a state of wisdom before acting. Season of Life awareness will be required of you as you evolve as well. In other words, as your circumstances continue to change in your life, you may find that a new Performance Motivator™ may become dominant. It is not unusual to move through the Boundary Balancer season, where that motivator takes more of a back seat and into a new one that becomes the more dominant motivator for you and your needs ahead.

Deliberate awareness, continued curiosity, and the willingness to have honest discussions with yourself will be how you will make decisions that you will truly be proud of, as they will be aligned with what's most important to you.

What Boundary Balancers Need:

- They need to know that the partnership agreement is a win-win. They want to bring everything they can to the table, knowing that the company is truly willing to accommodate their Performance Motivator.
- Support in accommodating their needs—their top life priority.
- Honesty and transparency from their employer with challenges or issues that arise.

- Flexibility without fear or guilt attached.
- Clear guidelines and expectations of responsibilities so everyone can measure for success.
- Support with other teammates who may or may not agree or believe in the fairness of the arrangements.
- Coaching and support through prioritizing tasks.
- Continued communication as the seasons of life continue to evolve.

CHAPTER 10

The Impact Player

Impact Player

My First Hire: Tom, the Incredible A+ Construction Manager's Story

My first hire, the incredible A+ construction manager, Tom, was a clear *Impact Player*—lucky for me. As I mentioned at the beginning of the story, he didn't earn any more working for me than he did at his previous job; in fact, in some ways, he probably made less, at least in the beginning. Tom was never at risk of losing his job there, and he loved working hard, so he didn't really care about having time off or work-life balance at that time in his life. What he was tired of was doing the same thing over and over for the same people in the same way. He wanted to contribute his part, but it felt like a small impact on the massive numbers that the company was already generating. His contributions and efforts were important, but he just didn't feel like he was making a real, needle-moving impact any longer. This was his chance. He wanted to bring significant impact, make a mark, and be an integral part of something greater. Tom knew he could be a key player as my right hand, and that was far more powerful than what he was getting where he was—and he did. Our company was set up for the best opportunity for success because of everything he brought.

Clark the CFO's Story

We all know that in the high-achieving corporate world, numbers hold the key to success, and our CFO, Clark, stood out for his numeric superpowers. So much so that he earned himself the nickname "Clark Kent."

We've known each other since our early corporate career days. His two daughters are just as brilliant as he is, and, as he likes to say, they are as beautiful as his wife.

But underneath all his kindness and brilliance, something was going on with him!

One typical Wednesday morning, I was strolling through the office as I normally do, exchanging good mornings and catching up with the team. In the kitchen, our morning hang-out spot, everyone was chatting and laughing as they normally do—except Clark. He just wasn't acting like himself. But I didn't draw any attention to it.

Later, I got to work diving into one of our latest, really important projects and realized I needed Clark's input. As we dove into things, he was still in a funk, so I asked, "Clark, what's up?!" And it all came out. He asked me about a corporate conference call where he wasn't on the invite list. He was left wondering, with all his insight and wisdom, how in the world he'd been left out of it.

I realized there was a miscommunication along the way, quickly explained what happened, and straightened things out without any hesitation. And all was well.

But in that moment, the past collided with the present. Memories of our past working relationship came rushing back to me from when Clark was the right-hand man in driving the division's strategies. A shake-up in upper management altered his standing, and Clark decided to begin searching for new opportunities—despite no change in title or compensation.

The revelation hit me: Clark is an Impact Player, someone who thrives on playing a pivotal role in shaping the future of the company. He craved a seat at the table where decisions of great consequence and significance were made. Without that, it would be "just a job."

While I didn't realize it at the time, I managed to say all the right things when recruiting Clark to join our team. Had I not, he would have continued looking elsewhere until he found what he was seeking.

Knowing this changed everything. As a leader, I made certain that Clark's strengths were maximized, and we pushed him more than he'd ever been pushed before. He thrived, and the value he brought to the success of our company was priceless.

Let me be clear: Clark does not question whether he will be paid well. He is confident in his value and what he is worth in the market, and he doesn't question it. Yet, for an Impact Player, even a high-level executive CFO Impact Player, it was never really about the money.

William the Transaction Coordinator's Story

William and I go way back. We worked together in my first position in my corporate career many years ago, before I knew anything about the industry. William was a transaction and closing coordinator before getting married. Throughout his career, he decided that he wanted to pursue sales, where the income potential is much greater.

He was an instant success, with his easy-going and calm, trusting personality. He achieved goals and exceeded the plan year over year, steadily and consistently. When it came time to hire a sales professional for my new company, I immediately thought of William.

That was a success as well. I was fortunate that he brought the ability to sell and the background of the transactional and closing aspects of the sale—an incredible mix of talent that didn't exist elsewhere in the market, as far as I was aware. He was dedicated, committed, and made a mark on the company as our first salesperson, carrying us into the success we saw in our future.

Along the way, William's personal life changed as his son got older and started playing baseball. He was missing tournaments due to the weekend demands of the sales position, so he again became my closing coordinator, and that's when it became clear how much of an Impact Player William had always been. It might be easy to think that he became a Boundary Balancer when life's seasons changed—that was the mistake I made at first, too. But I was wrong. It became clear that he was an Impact Player. He took on every part of his job with great care and ownership. He would not delegate any responsibilities to grow. He wanted to do everything himself, do it right, and be certain that I and the company had it "exactly the way it needed to be."

When he went on vacation or had any baseball tournaments to attend with his son, he wouldn't teach anyone else how to do his tasks and was known to pack his printer in his car so he could do 100% of the work on his own, without fail, remotely (long before work was really done remotely very easily!). As we continued to grow and his workload became far too large, he refused and avoided helping me to hire anyone new for the tasks and would not train anyone else to take on the responsibilities—even the simplest ones. With some good coaching and guidance, we overcame it all, but William was my very first example of how an Impact Player operates when it's their Performance Motivator.

Candace the National VP of Sales and Marketing's Story

Candace is a dedicated leader who manages a large sales team for a national company. She is happily married with a bonus daughter in middle school and a sweet two-year-old son. She and her husband divide and conquer to manage parenting, household responsibilities, and their thriving careers. Like many leaders in roles like hers, the reason she does what she does is that she wants to help others, make their jobs and lives better, and bring value to the company. Candace is an Impact Player who defines her success each day by whether she can account for the ways she contributed and impacted her team for the company's benefit.

As can be the case with any of the Performance Motivator™ types, the need to satisfy this drive may trump most other things in her life. She went so long rescheduling doctor appointments that she eventually gave up and decided to plan on scheduling them again "when there's more time for it." She had gone 2.5 years without a check-up or a dentist appointment. Vacations are limited, and she most recently canceled a family beach trip because it was just going to be too much work to go with two kids, especially when she was already exhausted from everything she had been pushing herself to do at work. She saw the daily tasks of making dinner together as a family, playing with her two-year-old on the floor, and helping her middle schooler with homework as obligations and exhausting chores. Her Performance Motivator™ as an Impact Player was tremendously valuable to the company; however, it was taking a big toll on her life in every possible way.

As you can imagine, her lack of self-care and the stress she was experiencing were actually creating the opposite effect, limiting her ability to maximize the impact she so desperately wanted to achieve and bring. Through several years of coaching, Candace not only created more success and impact for herself in her personal life but also achieved a big promotion, allowing her to bring an even greater impact to the company.

It might be easy to mistake her for a Success Seeker. Certainly, some of her traits and actions might suggest that. However, for Candace, she was *never* looking for the climb or the promotion. It was never her objective or goal. She was always consistently focused on impact and value, bringing the most she could to improve and attain greater results for the company. In fact, when the possibility of putting her name in the hat for the promotion was first brought to her, she declined, thinking that the additional responsibilities and title would not allow her to bring her maximum impact to the team. The promotion came as a result of her ability to own her Performance Motivator™ and recognize where it was serving her and where it was not so she could become even more effective and powerful in her entire life. This is a stark difference.

As an Impact Player

You are clearly a leader and have a strong desire to be part of the strategy and direction of the company. Because you appreciate being recognized, you put yourself in a position to bring high-quality data and value to impact success. You work hard and aren't afraid to work long hours to meet any demands that the company may deem necessary for the success of your business plan and goals. You are a dedicated and servant-style leader who proves your value repeatedly. This has brought great success to you along the way and is your style and approach in business. You've created habits that serve you well in achieving success and meeting your goals. Others likely see you as a role model, leader, mentor, or teacher—each of these serves both you and the company well.

This means that when all things are equal, you will always lean toward choosing the place that fills this Performance Motivator™ for you. This likely also means that when you have this Performance Motivator™ met, you are loyal and, therefore, unlikely to be lured away easily (even when things start to become less equal or just different). When it comes down to it, if Company

B will pay you a little bit more but doesn't allow you to bring your value and to be recognized for your efforts and expertise (possibly even showing you the red flags for where you would be handcuffed in doing so), it's not going to be the choice you make when Company A is fulfilling what you care about most but possibly cannot pay quite as much. Your *why* for getting up each morning is to bring that value, not for a couple of extra bucks!

Impact Player Words of Caution

As with any blessing we have in life, it can also be a curse for us too. While this has been a habit that has proven successful for you in many ways, it can also limit your growth and progress too. As the seasons of your life change and your priorities change, these habits can get in the way of creating what you want next. It's easy to fall into the habits that have always worked, even though they are not the ones that are really serving you toward your next level of goals. Being very clear about your priorities in each season of your life is critical in your decision-making as you now understand that you have a core Performance Motivator™ that will play into it for you. Your desire and need for recognition may sometimes cloud your judgment as you make decisions and operate throughout the day.

Sometimes value and recognition will not be available to you from others, and it will be up to you to recognize that it doesn't mean anything about you—or them. It may also be hard to see that you are having an impact when, in fact, you are. Sometimes it is hard to see it, so you'll need to trust that you are bringing value even when it may not be apparent at the moment. You will need to decide whether to give that validation to yourself and trust the process, or to allow it to drive you toward making emotional decisions that don't lead you down the path you really want to achieve. In other words, becoming frustrated, disappointed, or angry over being left off a meeting attendee list might drive you to operate in ways that don't serve you—such as how you are acting toward others, how you are showing up, or even making decisions to quit or change jobs as a result.

None of these decisions would have been made from your best place and best fuel—which usually means you could regret them later. These flags are there for a reason and serve to help you pay attention and ask questions, but then it is up to you to manage yourself in a state of wisdom before acting. This is how you will make decisions that you will truly be proud of, as they will be aligned with what's most important to you.

Carefully thought-out and deliberate boundaries will be important for you to both establish and honor. You may find it easy to give and give of yourself, work long hours, and be the first to arrive and the last to leave in an effort to bring the value and impact you so desire. However, recognizing that boundaries and balance will allow you to maximize that effort is key to achieving the impact you truly want. The impact you can bring is infinite, and the "work" of that will never cease. It is impossible to accomplish everything in one 24-hour day, one 7-day workweek, or even an entire year.

There is no rush. Patience and mindfulness of the ultimate goal are your allies here. This includes weighing the best ways and methods that will lead you to be able to bring maximum impact. A new and different role, laterally or a promotion, may be the best way to bring the most impact to the company, the team, and the goals the company wishes to achieve. Be cautious not to discount all the possibilities that may be placed in front of you as an Impact Player. Your awareness and constant curiosity of your Performance Motivator™ will serve you well in your decision-making.

Delegating tasks and training others may be a challenge for you. You might think that doing so means you are bringing less value or that you will become less necessary, impactful, or valuable. This is not true. Your value will actually erode if you continue to operate in this manner, as you will only bring less and less of your very best to the company and your role. What makes you less valuable is when you continue to do tasks that others are capable of handling instead of elevating yourself to what is next.

It will be important for you to recognize that while you know what motivates you, this motivation will not always apply to others. Assuming that others operate the same way you do will cause you to become disconnected from your peers and direct reports. It's important to understand that being an Impact Player is just one of the Six Performance Motivators, so you are only part of 17% of the whole picture. If you attempt to manage and motivate others the same way you would yourself, you will not connect with the other 83% of people. Most of us relate to and speak to others the way we want to be treated and spoken to. That is how we are designed. However, this is an opportunity for you to get to know others better, learn about them, and understand how they are motivated differently. Awareness is key! Your challenge now is to learn more about all six Performance Motivators and to get to know the members of your team better. Once we see that each of us is driven by a Performance Motivator™ that must be met, we have so much opportunity to speak to, motivate, retain, and create workplaces and cultures that serve both the people and the company's needs best. *It's Never About the Money* is the concept to become mindful of as we work through this process.

What Impact Players Need:

- They want to be in the know—kept up to speed and included whenever possible in decision-making and updates. Communication is key!
- They want to be relied upon for what they bring to the table and recognized for the importance of the skills they bring to drive change.
- They want to see the results of their work—what changed, improved, or succeeded in attaining the next level of success as a result?
- They need encouragement and guidance (likely even permission, or possibly even more firmly- insistent direction) in delegating and

training others so they can elevate themselves and bring the most value to their role for the company.

- Reminding them to respect boundaries and encouraging them to create a balance in their lives will allow them to bring their best to the company. You are unlikely to need to worry that an Impact Player is going to slack off or take advantage.
- Continued communication and direction to best utilize the power of their impact throughout the company to the best of their ability.

CHAPTER 11

The Structure Wiz

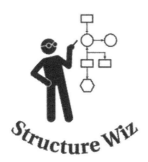

Harry the Estimator's Story

Harry's story is heartwarming. His arrival at our company was a significant event, as he had left his previous position with a competitor. His reasons for leaving were deliberate: He found his previous role overwhelmingly demanding, chaotically organized, and with a manager who struggled to handle it all.

In the market, Harry was well known for his exceptional skills. Recognizing the treasure we had acquired, I considered promoting him to Senior Estimator. This would unlock his potential to train and guide others, oversee the department, and spearhead special projects—a perfect alignment of his talents and our needs, accompanied by a well-deserved compensation increase.

Excited by this idea, I discussed it with his department manager, only to learn that Harry had politely declined. I was confused; I thought he'd be excited. But his manager shed light on Harry's journey. Once upon a time, Harry had aspired to climb the corporate ladder, investing countless efforts in learning, gaining certifications, and pursuing higher education. His hard work propelled him to success.

However, his manager explained that Harry now had new priorities. Harry had recently married later in life and welcomed his disabled mother-in-law, who was suffering from MS, into their home with open arms and utmost compassion. Caring for her and focusing on his new family life were now what fulfilled him the most.

Harry found contentment and fulfillment in his current role. Climbing the career ladder no longer held the same appeal. Instead, he wanted security, certainty, and the structure to rely on his position and income to remain stable. His previous company had overlooked this change in his life, assigning him more responsibilities even when he declined a similar promotion, which led to his decision to leave. Their "big growth and exciting opportunities" (which typically leave Success Seekers drooling with excitement) translated to full-on risk and fear for Harry.

Recognizing this, we chose a different path. We let go of the idea of advancement, and he found comfort in knowing that he could thrive within the structure and security of his current position. As a *Structure Wiz,* the security of a consistent and reliable income that he could depend on with minimal risk was his core emotional driver, his Performance Motivator™. Don't upset the apple cart: Keeping things steady and consistent, maintaining his family's health insurance, and ensuring that the retirement fund is maximized, secure, and in place—these were his only priorities. Life is an unpredictable journey, and our priorities evolve over time through the seasons of our lives. When these changes go unrecognized, like in Harry's case, people will seek the security they need elsewhere. For a Structure Wiz like him: *it was never about the money.*

Dana the Accountant's Story

From an early age, Dana knew that he wanted to create a career that would provide the income and security he desired as a successful CPA. He built his career with a large corporate organization with a long-standing reputation and a proven track record of success. He had achieved an incredibly strong compensation package at the firm and built a solid resume for himself, securing a stable future.

As with everything in life, our priorities and circumstances change. Shortly after marrying his very successful and driven wife and the birth of their second child, they decided it made the most sense for him to stay home with the kids. He would manage the finances and logistics of the home as his new career. Upon his departure, he was faced with several important financial decisions, one of which was whether or not to cash in his company stock. He had the choice to take what it was worth now and walk away with it in his pocket, or to leave it and let it grow for the future. This is where his Structure Wiz motivations came into play: security, risk aversion, and fear of loss. Based on these priorities, Dana chose to cash in the stocks and move on.

Fast forward a decade, and guess what happened? His colleagues from that firm have stocks worth millions. Even Dana knew, as we discussed the different Performance Motivator™ types, that being a Structure Wiz was his dominant motivator during that season of his life. Dana and I had many discussions and sessions surrounding this topic. One could argue that it's his personality to be a Structure Wiz. There are personality traits here that others may recognize in themselves, too. And Dana would certainly lean in that direction in many situations. However, in this season of his life, it was a far more dominant driver for him. He admitted that he would have made a different decision had he either been in different circumstances at that time or if he had taken the time to examine his reasons for making those decisions and determine whether or not he liked making them from a place of fear and insecurity.

Neither of those things happened, and it's water under the bridge now. And there is certainly always the argument that he could have lost that money just as easily as he could have made it had he made a different decision. The main point of focus here is that, in that particular season of his life, he was operating as a Structure Wiz, with security, minimizing risk, and maximizing all he had already earned as his main emotional drivers and needs that required satisfying.

As a Structure Wiz

Security, conservative decision-making, and being risk-averse are some of the overall dominant traits that drive you right now. You are a rock-solid and reliable member of the team. Everyone knows what to expect from you. You are dependable and produce high-quality work. Your job is very important to you, and you bring your best value in everything you do. You are also very clear on your boundaries and how you want to live your life from a balanced standpoint. You give yourself fully at work and at home. So, when you leave the office, you don't take work home with you and have no interest in being available by phone, text, or email after hours, as this would interfere with your personal priorities. If asked to do something outside the norm, you are a willing team player, but this is not your usual way of operating, and it is not how you want to work regularly. You want to be recognized for what you bring and are very proud of the quality of work you produce, and it is important to you that others see that too. However, it isn't for the purpose of climbing, achieving, or proving anything to anyone, but for the stability and security that you seek in your position. You are valued in your organization and do not seek change as long as the arrangement continues to serve everyone. You want to contribute to serving your life in the best way you can.

While you are willing to learn, taking on new challenges and changing the methods you know and love is not necessarily desirable for you, as they are not your main emotional driver or priority at this time. You may see big growth and change as a risk to the company or your own position's security. You don't thrive in the chaos of growth and scale and prefer a slow and steady, controlled environment that is managed as such. While you are a driven, focused, and hard worker, you do not thrive on new challenges, innovations, or big improvements where you are in the driver's seat or responsible for their success. This means that when all things are equal, you will always lean toward choosing the place that fulfills this Performance Motivator™ for you. This also likely means that when this Performance Motivator™ is met, you are loyal and, therefore, unlikely to be lured away easily (even when things start to become less equal or just different).

When it comes down to it, if Company B will pay you a little bit more but is unclear about responsibilities and expectations or requires out-of-the-box hours or changes, it's not going to be the choice you make—when Company A is fulfilling what you care about most but possibly cannot pay quite as much. Your *why* is based on contributing, bringing high-quality and reliable work, and the stability of a dependable, consistent, and secure position—not a few extra bucks.

Structure Wiz Words of Caution

As with any blessing we have in life, it can also be a curse. While this habit has brought you success in many ways, it can also limit your growth and progress. As the seasons of your life change and your priorities shift, these habits can get in the way of creating what you want next. It's easy to fall into habits that have always worked, even though they may not be serving you toward your next level of goals. Being very clear about your priorities in each season of your life is critical in your decision-making as you now understand that you have a Performance Motivator™ that plays into it for you.

There will be times when shifts and changes occur that may test and require more of you. When leaders see high quality and great contribution, it is only natural that they want to expand on it and gain more of it for the organization through challenges of change. Awareness is key. At the end of the day, changes, growth, scale, and improvements do not threaten your security or abilities in your role in any way. You have just interpreted them to mean that for you. Trust that you will always be in the driver's seat for your decision-making and choices in your roles, career path, and financial opportunities. It will be up to you to recognize that it doesn't mean anything about you—or them. You will need to decide whether to be open-minded and consider new perspectives and how questioning some of the boundaries you have put in place for yourself may not be serving you, or to allow it to drive you toward making emotional decisions that don't lead you down the path you really want to achieve.

In other words, becoming frustrated, disappointed, or fearful over a change in direction or a decision or demand might lead you to act in ways that don't serve you—from how you interact with others, how you show up, or even making decisions to quit or change jobs as a result. None of these decisions would have been made from your best place and best fuel, which usually means you could regret them later. These flags are there for a reason and serve for you to pay attention and ask questions. But then it is up to you to operate from a state of wise leadership before acting. This is how you will make decisions that you will truly be proud of, as they will be aligned with what's most important to you.

What the Structure Wiz Needs:

- Communication is always key—being aware of who you are talking to and understanding not just what they need to hear, but how they need to hear it, can have a powerful impact on success.
- No matter what changes are on the horizon, the Structure Wiz needs to see how their involvement translates to security and minimizing risk. You need to show them this clearly.

- When recruiting, motivating, or attempting to retain a Structure Wiz, be cautious not to focus solely on future growth opportunities and scaling the big business plan without outlining why and how these changes have tremendous benefits and advantages for someone who prefers security and minimal risk. Don't scare them away with your excitement for growth!

- If you are a Structure Wiz Leader, being aware of this will be powerful in how you lead, recruit, and motivate a team likely filled with other Performance Motivator™ types who thrive on things that you may not. You will need to be aware of these differences and find the best way to communicate with others.

- Structure Wiz individuals need to be seen and valued for the wizards they are while also recognizing that their emotional drive for security and minimal change dominates their regular decision-making and cautious, steady approach.

- If they don't want to grow or change, pushing or forcing them may risk driving them away from you and the company entirely.

CHAPTER 12

The Change Champion

You don't have to be Florence Nightingale, Nelson Mandela, or Mother Theresa to be a *Change Champion*.

Change Champions can come in the form of millennials who want to change the world, our children who have limitless opportunities to make things better, or even individuals who strive to revolutionize the world around them!

They may be like my best friend's daughter, who has been out of college for two years and is a junior project manager, doing things like spreadsheet and software tracking for leads on big projects. She could do this kind of work for anyone, anywhere, and make a lot more money, by the way. But she has a passion for wind and energy pursuits, and she has chosen to work for a company whose tagline is "Results Through Meaningful Impact." I watched the video on the homepage of their website—it was moving. I'm pretty sure it was the primary reason she chose to work for them.

Or maybe they want to work for a female-owned company or leader who stands for change and empowerment, paving the way for wide-open possibilities and opportunities!

Change Champions have taught me that what we stand for, or even what we stand against as companies, is important not just to our clients, but to our team members and the cultures we create as well. Making the world a better place in some way is far more valuable to them than financial gains being their primary focus. Because for the Change Champions, *it's never about the money!*

Michelle's Change Champion Story

At this latest stage in my career, I have successfully built myself to the point of being able to choose what I want to do and what I am most passionate about. My circumstances have changed dramatically, and I am in the fortunate position to pursue what truly matters to me now.

At this point, I am the ultimate example of *It's Never About the Money.* There is purpose and passion in my desire to support leaders through their biggest challenges and struggles. I can relate to being in your position at some point along the way in my career. Whether it be the frustrations of managing people on the team, the anxiety of not being able to get it all done, the pressures of the demands your company and bosses may be putting on you, burnout, lack of balance, or feeling like you will never get out from under everything on your plate—whatever your challenge or struggle, I can relate because I have been there. I want to be the life raft, support, or resource, or whatever you need to get you where you want to go, to the point where you feel confident, empowered, in control of your destiny, and armed with all the tools you need to create a career and life that are filled with joy and success.

And our world needs better leaders. Look around. Some of those in leadership positions are not so great. Whether that be in the corporate world, the small or mid-sized business world, or the political world, I want to be an agent of change toward building better, stronger leaders in this world. As I've said, Season of Life is key here. I am now a Change Champion. I began as a Success Seeker, made a Tribe Thinker stop along the way, had a Boundary Balancer phase while my kids finished school, and am now powerfully positioned in Change Champion drive mode. I hope I can help you achieve your dream, and in turn, you will be helping me achieve mine as well.

I still have extensive involvement and drive to run my businesses and partner with others in theirs to help them scale or operate at their best efficiency. I am still a die-hard entrepreneur and love business and working. Just because I am a Change Champion now does not mean I don't appreciate business, success, and hard work. But my passion, my emotional motivator, is for change and better leadership, for better-run companies, for a human element and culture enhancement that allows for better businesses, better companies, service, quality, and improved bottom lines. That is the change I champion now at a deeper level.

While our home-building company wasn't necessarily founded by Change Champions at the time, our charitable efforts were enormous based on our philosophies of giving back to the community that we served and who served us. Relationships. That was a consistent mission in the way we operated from Day 1- even when we were struggling the most. Beginning our first year in business, a portion of our sales was donated to the local fire dept and the local elementary school library. Our efforts only built upon that from there, having participated in charity build projects and Habitat for Humanity.

Then in 2014, our Team built the Duke Children's Miracle Home, a yearlong fundraising and building event that allowed us to donate $200,000 to the Duke Children's Hospital—a project that bonded our team at a level that no other project we did could match. This was true to who we were as a company, as a team, and how we gave to our community in every way possible—together. This mission and project served each of us, regardless of our Performance Motivator™. Our Change Champion team members were further cemented and invested in our mission and future as a result.

Alaina's Change Champion Story

I want to share one last Change Champion story with you. My friend Alaina has built an entire company culture driven by Change Champions. She founded a home-building company with a purpose and a mission—proving that a home-building company can change the world. The passion projects that her company has pursued over the years are remarkable.

Every home Alaina's company builds pays it forward through their giveback program. A portion of the proceeds from each home they build is donated to a fund the company uses to further its mission of changing the world. The company has built homes with local Habitat for Humanity affiliates and has gifted three homes to Gold Star Families (immediate family members of a U.S. military service member who died in the line of duty) to honor the sacrifice of their husbands, fathers, wives, mothers, and heroes. They have participated in designing and constructing affordable housing for people struggling with serious mental illness in partnership with a local nonprofit. The team constructed tiny homes as a demonstration project in hopes that other builders would volunteer for similar opportunities to confront the affordable housing crisis.

Alaina says giving back is how her company fulfills a promise to be good stewards of their success. Taking one person's dream of homeownership realized and paying it forward to make it possible for another person's dream of homeownership.

Because of this mission-driven culture, she continues to attract more incredible people who have joined because of it. They believe in the mission, passion, and purpose that the company aspires to and lives each day.

There are many small, mid-, and large-sized companies in every industry that have missions and passions that drive their cultures. They, in turn, attract employees, partners, investors, and clients who join them solely for those missions. Don't underestimate the power of the Change Champions in our world.

Because for the Change Champions… *it's never about the money.*

About Change Champions

Your passion and drive are focused on the greater good and the bigger picture. Standing for something larger than yourself is what fulfills you, and you are focused on making this an important part of the culture of your life and where and for whom you choose to work. You bring an energy and perspective that others appreciate and want to get behind in your mission and cause. You bring a sense of community to the group through your passion and drive. This adds a richness to organizations and helps shape their cultures. Bravo! This means that when all things are equal, you will always lean toward choosing the place that fills this Performance Motivator™ for you. This likely also means that when you have this Performance Motivator™ met, you are loyal and, therefore, unlikely to be lured away easily (even when things start to become less equal or just different).

When it comes down to it, if Company B will pay you a little bit more but doesn't stand for something you believe in or doesn't give back or have a passion and mission toward something outside of itself, it's not going to be the choice you make—when Company A is fulfilling what you care about most but possibly cannot pay quite as much. Your *why* for getting up each morning is to stand behind a mission or passion for something greater, not for money.

Change Champion Words of Caution

As with any blessing in life, it can also be a curse. While this habit has brought you success in many ways, it can also limit your growth and progress. As the seasons of your life and your priorities change, these habits may hinder your ability to create what you want next. It's easy to fall back on familiar habits, even when they are no longer serving you in reaching your next level of goals. Being very clear about your priorities in each season of your life is critical in your decision-making, as you now understand that you have a core Performance Motivator™ that will influence your actions.

Your desire and need to stand for something and believe in the mission may sometimes cloud your judgment as you make decisions and operate throughout the day. Sometimes, things will not look the way you want them to, especially if you are not in a leadership position to have all the perspectives and decision-making responsibilities that others may have. It will be up to you to recognize that it doesn't reflect anything about you—or them. Don't lose sight of the big picture; be sure to establish clear goals and objectives, define success, and show how success is what allows the change and mission to be carried out. No matter what choices you make, even if that means you venture outside of the Change Champion Performance Motivator… none of that has to mean that change, passion, mission, and all the things you care about would go by the wayside. Your Performance Motivator™ can change without sacrificing the causes and missions you care about—you still get to be you, no matter what. Give yourself the gifts of curiosity, awareness, and the permission to evolve naturally based on the seasons of your life.

Don't forget that in business, generating revenue and minimizing expenses are the only ways to be profitable. And being profitable is what allows the company to have maximum change and impact. If the company goes out of business due to irresponsible spending or reduced revenues and customers, it won't matter what the company stands for anymore if the company is no longer standing at all. Creating business acumen for yourself at this time will allow you to maximize the change you wish to see!

You will need to decide whether to be open-minded and willing to see other perspectives or to allow it to drive you toward making emotional decisions that don't lead you down the path you really want to achieve. In other words, becoming frustrated, disappointed, or angry over a change in direction or a decision that is not aligned with your expectations or beliefs might cause you to act in ways that don't serve you—from how you interact with others to how you show up, or even making decisions to quit or change jobs as a result. None of these decisions would be made from your best place and best mindset—which usually means you could regret them later. These flags are there for a reason and serve as a reminder to pay attention and ask questions. But then, it is up to you to manage yourself with wisdom before acting. This is how you will make decisions that you will truly be proud of, as they will be aligned with what's most important to you, and the change you wish to honor.

Change Champion Needs

Communication is key: Understand who you are talking to and how they need to hear what you have to say in order to address their *why*.

I am often told that managing Change Champions, especially in the non-profit sector, is challenging due to their extreme focus on passion, the change mission, or charity, yet they often lack the skill sets or business acumen necessary to bring success. Showing them how it is all related is key. Teach them the connection between achieving their goals and accomplishing all the goals.

- **Celebrate success**: The best way to celebrate the success of your impact is to measure it. Staying focused on the value and impacts that are achieved goes a long way—even with small steps. Measure and discuss them.

- **Follow through**: Claiming your mission and passion is one thing; following through on them is another. Ensure you have a plan in place to achieve the goals you wish to reach.

- **Significance**: Change Champions need to know that their work is valuable and significant to the greater good and cause.

CHAPTER 13

Let's Build! Pulling It All Together

While emotional drivers can be categorized, the reasons why individuals have emotional motivations vary widely. We don't need to be therapists, coaches, or doctors here—that is most certainly outside of your scope as a Manager or Leader. And unless they are asking for your help, it's really not any of our business at all, nor our job to show them or change them. I would not want my manager to make the decision without my permission to try to coach me or change me, and I'm guessing you wouldn't either. So that is most certainly not an objective of this information. People get to choose to be motivated by whatever they want, and they get to decide if they want to explore the reasons behind it. Their self-awareness is not what's important here. The only thing you really need to know is *what* their motivation is, not *why* it is.

These six Performance MotivatorTM types are the emotional needs, drives, or desires that direct actions to satisfy those needs, drives, or desires:

Success Seekers like my early self or like many of you may relate to.

 Impact Players like Clark Kent.

 Structure Wizzes like Heartwarming Harry.

 Boundary Balancers like Saint Bonnie.

 Tribe Thinkers like Boomerang Bob.

 All the Change Champions who seek "results through meaningful impact."

No matter how much you relate to one or more of these, and you likely will, there is only *one* primary motivator in *this* season of your life. Not last season—*this* season. It is your emotional need that must be satisfied.

It is your deal-breaker. Your hard stop. Your non-negotiable. An absolute.

Awareness is the beginning, and the willingness to ask incredible questions of yourself, your team, your peers, and even your bosses to find the real answers—*that* is mastery!

I'm often asked whether someone can change their Performance Motivator™ if they don't like it. The short answer is yes. But the more important answer lies in the process you need to go through to do it. If we are being driven by a motivator that comes from an emotional place, we can always change it. First, we must understand it and acknowledge it fully. But in the end, in order to change our emotion about it, we must first either change the circumstances that were the root of it, *or* we must change our belief or thought about that circumstance. This requires coaching, sometimes professionally guided therapy, thought work, and time, because it is natural to default to the thoughts and beliefs that created the emotions that brought you to this Performance Motivator™ in the first place. It is, therefore, natural that you will continue to take action—or *not* take action—that supports the original Performance Motivator™. There's no hiding from what truly and authentically motivates you. However, because these motivators are emotionally driven, the best news is that they can be driven by you and your authentic choices—your decisions.

Most importantly: There are no right or wrong Performance Motivators. Judging them causes us to miss the point. It's much more difficult to change someone than it is to meet them where they are and go from there.

It's not about being everything to everyone. It's about showing how you can be the right thing for them, how what you already have and what you already offer satisfies exactly what they are looking for. You don't have to change anything you offer if you don't want to. You just have to show them how what you already have is exactly what they need and want.

Understand the things that attract and are applicable to all six Performance MotivatorTM types. You already have something unique and special in your company culture that can speak to each of these Performance MotivatorTM types. Applying them to each individual is the key to creating loyalty and thriving for true long-term success.

When there are issues (performance or otherwise), conflicts, or problems, it's most likely due to someone's Performance Motivator™ being at risk, threatened, or possibly even changing altogether! Any of these will create changes in how they are acting, showing up, performing, or possibly even reacting in the workplace.

Frustrated with your entire team not performing? It might be the same answer for everyone, but the odds are good that it's a different answer for each of them. Sometimes, there are larger issues that cause low morale or concern, but even when that is true, it's important to remember that each individual only cares about how that larger issue is affecting them personally and in their own lives. You guessed it—their Performance Motivator™ is top of mind and needs to be satisfied and resolved again. Either you as a leader can help them do that, or they will do it themselves and make decisions to resolve it on their own. But it will not just go away—humans will work and struggle to ensure their Performance Motivator™ is always satisfied.

Application Case Study: Tara's Design Firm

Tara is the owner of a very successful interior design firm. She started her own company after working as an employee at a large, local firm and quickly created success for herself. She attributes her success to some very simple principles: creating great relationships with people, doing what she said she would do (aka living up to her word), and providing great quality work.

She is an excellent designer, and before she knew it, the growth of her success followed. The Success Seeker in Tara found ways to create a unique niche, and her designs became recognizable, not just in her local community, but, with the help of social media, widely known throughout the region and, eventually, the entire nation. Tara's firm was sought after, and her client list became both long and high-profile, something Tara had strived to accomplish since the beginning. (You can see how Structural Footing #2—Company USP—is being formed here)

Tara's next step was adding people to help complete the work she had in front of her. *If only I could just clone myself,* she would think. Tara hired some other great designers to join her team, and her success continued. The only problem was that Tara was great at creating success and getting design

120

business, but she had no experience in leading or managing people. She quickly learned that if she wanted to grow her business, she needed to grow herself to become the leader she needed to be—for her business and for the people who worked for her.

Yet despite her efforts to motivate her team, Tara found herself frustrated with them. They didn't arrive at work early like she did each day. They would leave for long lunches rather than working at their desks while eating, at least occasionally, to meet project deadlines. They were constantly disputing working in the office and wanted to continue their pandemic work-from-home arrangements. They left at precisely 5 p.m. on the dot each day, not a second past. They just didn't have the hunger and drive that she had for success.

Tara gave great speeches to motivate the team, expressing her passion for the purpose and vision of the company. She created more team-related opportunities to connect and worked hard to improve the overall culture. These efforts did have a significant impact on the team's overall productivity and energy.

Yet, there was still an element of drive and motivation that Tara couldn't pinpoint how to fix. I asked Tara why she thought her people worked for her. She shared that she believed they loved working for a company with a big vision for where it could go and what it could become. My next question to her was: Why is that important to them? Why do they care about that? Would everyone have the same answer? That's when Tara understood the concept I have been referring to all along: *it's never about the money.* This rings true repeatedly in every example I have. Let's look at why…

Notice that as a Success Seeker, Tara's language, when she speaks to the team, aligns with what motivates her and what she cares about. Even when I asked her why they work for her, her answer was the one that would attract and motivate another Success Seeker.

It's important to emphasize that there is nothing incorrect with what Tara said or how she communicated her passion. She has been authentic and sincere in her communication, something that everyone appreciates in leaders. (One of the top leadership attributes I teach is the power of authenticity.) This is why she had some success with her team. They were likely moved, at some level, by seeing her passion and belief in what the team is capable of accomplishing. Big credit to Tara for rising to the occasion in her leadership journey toward creating an incredible culture and mission together!

The opportunity for potential is where I want to focus now. It is in our nature to speak to others the way we want to be spoken to. It's what we know and how we think, so it makes perfect sense that we would operate this way—it's completely natural and instinctual. We follow "the Golden Rule" for a reason, and this aligns perfectly with that approach. And this is an opportunity to evolve our leadership to the next level. Emotional leadership skills include, among many other things, the ability to see things from someone else's perspective or view. Finding empathy to understand how others are thinking, feeling, and what they care about most is the shift and up-level we are talking about in the concepts of this book. Recall Structural Footing #1-Relationships: Meet them where they are; create rapport and a level of understanding.

Does your employee love the vision of what can be accomplished because they are an *Impact Player,* and want to be a part of impacting that vision in the best way they can for you as the leader and for the company? What does that look like for that person? What is their role in creating it?

In Tara's case, she needed some power players by her side—people she trusted and confided in more closely—to bring them in and allow them to bring maximum impact for her and for them! Tara needed at least one Impact Player on her team.

Or are they a *Change Champion* who loves what you stand for, or against, in your values, mission, product, or service—and they want to shout your message from the rooftops about all that is possible because you and your company exist?

Tara's mission is to make a mark and leave a lasting legacy in the design field on a local and national scale. Change Champions love to get behind the purpose and mission, and Tara was doing it in new and innovative ways, unlike anywhere else in the country! Tara would benefit tremendously from encouraging the Change Champions on the team to carry that torch!

Maybe they are a *Structure Wiz,* and the vision translates to security and minimal risk for them. They want to contribute and be valued, but most importantly, they want to ensure that their job security and benefits are maximized as a result.

New and innovative ideas, big dreams and missions, and increases in business can send a Structure Wiz right out the door if you're not aware of where they sit on your team right now. But Tara needed the balance of having them on her team—people who would challenge and re-center her when needed. Tara is currently a Success Seeker, but she also had a bit of a Structure Wiz PM lurking in the background from her past experience of business during the Great Recession. She feared a repeat of that period, worried that taking big leaps could backfire on her. This is where a Structure Wiz can bring their logic and conservative, risk-averse approach to help Tara grow in a responsible manner that she likes.

They could be a Tribe Thinker, and the vision means to them that they get to be a part of an extended family and are on a team-driven mission to get there.

Tara was creating a culture of collaboration and improved service to clients through the tribe-like team that each client would experience. For the Tribe Thinkers on the team, celebrating this and the benefits to the clients attracts more Tribe Thinker-minded talent as well!

Maybe they are a Boundary Balancer and love all of it, but if any of it means interrupting the larger emotional priorities of their life, they won't be on board.

Having Boundary Balancers on your team is usually not your plan. It happens when you have incredible talent whom you value (or interview them to attract and hire), but they have limitations on how they fit into your overall process and standard routine and functionality. While you may not plan to add them, be willing to consider the possibilities of having them. Even if their job is an optional choice, the fact that they choose to have one is powerful and usually offers big benefits to you as the employer who gets to have this level of talent on the team. Tara needs to decide whether what someone brings is worth them also leaving at 4 p.m. each day—it's a choice, and it could be a great one.

You can see where the opportunities lie. How does it all translate to satisfying what they need and want most? When you can answer that question for your team, you are well on your way to maximizing their motivation for accomplishing your goals. They get to do it on their terms, for the reasons they believe in, and in ways that will satisfy them the most.

It can be so easy to fall into the trap of frustration and take other directions. Many leaders do. I have had several managers and leaders in my past who operated in more traditional ways:

- They try to force everyone to follow their rules, even the ones their employees don't like or agree with.
- They hold accountability sessions, write people up, or even put them on probation for not following the outlined rules.
- They continue to communicate in ways that alienate and disconnect them further from their employees.
- They just fire them, assuming they haven't quit on their own yet, or even force them out with other methods.

These leadership styles have become all too common in corporate settings and, unfortunately, are often the default for new managers or business owners too. They don't know another approach and have, at some point, probably worked for someone else who operated with these styles. Or they are just frustrated and can't figure out what to do to change it, so they default to trying to get others to change and "be better."

I would suggest that most people don't want to be forced to change, follow someone else's rules, or work for anyone who doesn't inspire them on another level—the emotional one. I know I don't, and I'm guessing you don't either.

If these old ways really don't get great results anyway... then I suggest we try a different approach.

Fortunately for Tara, she was able to make significant shifts when applying her Structural Footings of Relationship and Company USP to the concepts of the Performance Motivator System™. As a result, she hired a new Operations Manager (Impact Player), made some shifts in their processes, allowing everyone to contribute in the ways that served both them and the company best, and partnered with some national furniture connections as well to bring them even closer to the vision and future that Tara sought. Big congrats to her for these big shifts!

Application Case Study: Julia's Concrete Company

Julia owns a concrete footings company serving the vibrant new home construction industry. The concrete truck is critical to the operation of the company, and therefore, the concrete truck driver is ultimately critical too. Without them, you don't have a company at all. She shared with me that good-quality drivers are hard to find. They need to have a CDL (Commercial Driver's License), be trained to drive concrete trucks and have significant experience driving them. In one of our sessions together, she shared that they were "at the mercy of these guys."

I'm going to pause right there and share that whenever anyone tells me anything remotely like "We are at their mercy," "They can name their price," or "They get whatever they want," there are a few red flags that go off in my mind.

Any time a business is at the mercy of *one* sticking point that could make or break the business and cause it to fail, that's trouble. *No* business should be in that position, or it is a risky business to start. Even if there is some truth to that, operating from that belief will never get you, or them, a positive result. In essence, nothing good comes from thinking, believing, or deciding that "We are at their mercy." So, when I hear it, I immediately focus on that topic and how to unravel it and find the opportunities within it.

Julia had a tough week. It began on Monday when she found out that one of her lead truck drivers had quit. He was going to work for their main competitor in the business. She assumed it was for more money, and while we don't know whether that is true or not, for the sake of the story, we are going to assume that it probably is. They wished him well, but she reacted quickly and began the search for his replacement that week. Then, another bomb dropped later in the week: her second driver was arrested for a DUI and was likely going to lose his license, leaving them with no way to keep him. This truly put them in a lurch, jeopardizing their ability to service their business and maintain their clients. She and her team were in a panic.

She had big customers with very strict production build timelines, inspections scheduled, and soon-to-be-angry project managers and purchasing managers from the builders. Missing the start of a home means being behind and racing against the clock to ensure every stage of the build is completed on time. Corporations do not like missing completion dates, and customers do not like missing their closing and move-in dates.

Julia was under intense pressure—the worst possible place for a company owner to be when trying to make decisions. But Julia is smart and knows that staying calm and keeping a level head will accomplish much more than staying in panic mode. She stayed focused on finding replacements. Driver #3 pulled some extra hours that week and weekend. She told me they don't usually ask the drivers to work overtime because they are a family-owned company, and respect that.

Julia put on her recruiting hat and was able to hire an additional driver that week who started the following week. This helped relieve some of the pressure from the workload. These two actions helped alleviate the strain they were under.

But here's the twist: the following week, Driver #1—the first guy who quit, presumably for more money—came back! I told you that Julia is smart, knows how to keep a level head, and makes good decisions. That translated into her abilities in running her business too. Their concrete trucks are new. They are also very well maintained and have minimal maintenance needs, breakdowns, and issues. Their scheduling system is sophisticated and is updated throughout each day with building schedule changes. The drivers receive their schedules the day before to know where they are going, and their schedules are clear, firmed up, and properly outlined and mapped to be as efficient and accurate as possible. All this has several benefits: the drivers have a clear schedule they can plan their day around; they have minimal downtime and drive time, making their days efficient; they have high-quality vehicles that do not delay them or slow their work schedules down. All this means that drivers are consistently home by 6 p.m. every night with their families and rarely, if ever, work weekends.

Guess what competitor #1 has going on over there besides paying a little bit more to drivers? You guessed it—none of those things! That driver lasted just one week in that mess. Chaos, scheduling nightmares, getting home at 8 or 9 p.m. every night, problems with jobs not being ready for him, and having to backtrack his day—you name it! By the end of the week, following the panic that ensued the week prior, Julia now had three solid employees back on staff driving the concrete pump trucks. It had all worked out for the best.

I asked Julia what she thought the lessons were from all of this. I bet you can see some here too. One of the big takeaways is what we've been talking about all along, of course: Having regular quality conversations with your team members to understand what's important to them, show that you value them, and create strong relationships with them. (Structural Footing #1-Relationships) Whether they stay with you forever or leave one day doesn't matter. Building solid relationships will benefit you both during their time with you and after they leave.

Many times, we miss the advantages and benefits of what we offer as a company. Sometimes we don't realize that what we do regularly—because it's what we want—isn't necessarily what others offer. We just take it for granted that what we do is standard and not anything unique or special. But what I want to convey to you sincerely and urgently is that the culture you've created based on what you prioritize and value as a company is special. It is unique, and it is *not* necessarily what anyone else is doing (Structural Footing #2- Company USP).

Do your due diligence to understand what makes you different from the rest as a culture and as an employer—you may surprise yourself with those answers. You may realize how many things you do that are different and special, things that don't really cost much or can't have a dollar figure attached to them—mostly because they are somewhat priceless, at least for those who value them the most. And usually, it wasn't free for you to create it. *You* invested your time, energy, and resources into things that *you* cared about, which means others who care about them will value them too.

The nuances that can be applied to the concepts of the Performance MotivatorTM system are crucial. (The method you use to build your company - the Performance Motivator System™) Being familiar with what you offer as a company overall and then applying that to the Performance Motivator™ of your employees is what will take you to the next level. Had Julia had a conversation with the driver who quit at the time he left, she could have uncovered what was important to him. Ideally, she could have known more about how she stands out from the competition in advance, and she would have been having great conversations with him and the other employees well in advance to understand and highlight the value of what they offer as a company.

In a perfect world, the driver would never have been lured away by the competitor because he would have been fully aware of what he had and appreciated it. And even if a perfect world scenario didn't happen, there was an opportunity to have a conversation with him when he wanted to leave. Asking questions to understand more is always an opportunity to create a relationship, even if he ended up leaving anyway. Questions surrounding why he was leaving, whether he was familiar with the truck conditions there, if he was made aware of what his schedule would be like, and what kinds of hours he would be working—all of these would have allowed for more discovery and thought. All this opens a window for conversation that could create higher-quality discussions, allowing the employee to consider these factors.

Now again, he may have made the same decision—we don't know. But any of these routes offer an improved chance of preventing a great employee from leaving and possibly ever pursuing or considering the need to pay attention to suitors who come their way. These nuances are how the Performance MotivatorTM System can be put to work for you as a leader in new ways that gain you a loyal following and a team motivated to achieve goals. They value what you have valued and put into place for their benefit. They want to continue enjoying these benefits and working for a company that provides them. They want to protect these values as their own. They want to invite their friends to work for or buy from your company because they are loyal members of its fabric too. This is how you create incredible and award-winning places to work. Because—say it with me—*it's never about the money.*

Powerful questions are key, and even more vital is the skill of listening for the answers to them. Julia's saga, and even the story of Boomerang Bob, teach us that many times we can prevent the storms from beginning at all by showing employees how their true Performance Motivator™ is already being satisfied right here.

Application Case Study: The Doubting Captain

My husband and I own many businesses in a variety of industries. One of them is in the boating industry, and we employ a captain of a fishing charter vessel. About six years ago, based on the needs of the business at the time, we hired a part-time captain to oversee and care for the fleet of boats, as well as to run them as needed a few times throughout the year. We weren't looking to pay the salary expected of a typical highly qualified and experienced captain for this position since that level wasn't necessary or required for the needs we had available.

But we hit the jackpot anyway. We had a very experienced, highly qualified captain who wanted the position. We asked him why. He explained that he had been in demanding positions for his entire career. Now, he had a teenage boy at home, and he wanted to be there for him as he grew to become a young man. The months of long travel and only coming home for a weekend every month were not the lifestyle he wanted anymore, and this position would allow him to have the time with his family that he knew everyone wanted. He had become a Boundary Balancer, and it was the perfect win-win for all of us.

We all got to know each other really well, and I told him I was writing this book. He was very supportive and listened to the concept. Later, my husband had a conversation with him about it. The captain let him know that he didn't agree with my philosophy at all. "It's crazy that someone wouldn't go to work for the most money possible," he said. "Everyone makes decisions about where they work for the money."

My husband, by now converted to my perspective, replied, "Isn't it funny that the one telling me this is the person who is working for us for less money than he ever has before so he can work part-time to be with his family!"

When my husband later told me about the discussion, he said, "I couldn't keep my mouth shut: I had to point it out to him. His eyes widened. He knew exactly what I was saying was true!"

CHAPTER 14

Creating YOUR Signature Culture

As you've read my personal story and the many stories of others that I've shared, I believe you have likely begun to see how these concepts can be put into practice for yourself. The awareness of them is the beginning, and hopefully, I've provided you with a solid foundation to start looking at your company, culture, and team in a new way that allows you to maximize the bottom line of your company for everyone's benefit.

Here's how to get started creating your own Signature Culture.

We begin with our Two Structural Footings, allowing for The Foundation of the Performance Motivator System™ to be placed solidly that every company culture must rest upon:

Structural Footing #1: Relationships

Your community, your clients, your investors, your tradespeople, your service providers—everyone can be your partner. Build those relationships! And most importantly, focus on your employees and team!

As outlined in my story in Chapter 3, relationships are a key foundational component to creating what you (and they) want most and contributing to the long-term sustainability and financial health of the company for all to enjoy for many years to come.

Structural Footing #2: Company USP (Unique Selling Proposition)

Know who you are, own it, talk about it, and advertise it to the world. It starts with going through the exercise of understanding where your current culture stands and why it is that way. Making conscious choices about your values, mission, and what that fabric will look like together with your leadership team allows you to stand out from the rest and create a culture within your organization that appeals to everyone—both your customers and the talent in the market who will become your employees.

As discussed in Chapter 4, use those questions to help guide you toward creating something unique in the market! Ensure that your entire leadership team knows these concepts inside and out. Create a plan for utilizing key talking points within your organization and through your HR and marketing departments to highlight and talk about them consistently.

The Method: Applying the Performance Motivator™ System in Your Culture

Understand the makeup of your team through the Performance Motivator System™. I always encourage that the best practice toward creating your best quality and most accurate results is by following Structural Footing #1—building relationships. High-quality conversations between team leaders and employees have become a lost art. It is a skill that should be practiced and honed to create high-quality relationships, yet it is rarely used today.

Everyone wants to be heard, seen, and understood. Nobody wants to feel like a number. Most new hires have had their resumes fed through auto-screening chatbots, received auto-generated email responses, and had no path toward communicating with another human at all. Once hired and part of the team, the reality of the business kicks in: Business is busy and stressful, and there aren't enough people to get the jobs done, let alone train someone or get to know them. Corporate policies and red tape kick in, and you're lucky to get an annual review or sit down with a team leader at all. So we check the boxes that must be checked and move on to the next thing to stay on track. There are many benefits to these efficiencies, and in times of limited manpower, they have become necessary. However, we have lost sight of the value of genuine human interaction as a way to create more opportunities for ourselves—the benefits of this art form are immeasurable.

So, my strong plea to you as a leader is to spend the time during interviewing, hiring, onboarding, and throughout your team members' career paths to truly understand who they are and what motivates them. It takes time, and this understanding will evolve and build over the months and years ahead as you continue to follow this practice—but it is worth it. The quality of the results and the insight you will gain as you gather your information will allow you to truly lead through the Performance Motivator™ System much more accurately and far more intuitively. I can't stress that preference strongly enough!

However, if you fall into the category of being overworked and understaffed, or you really want to just get a jump start with your team, or perhaps if you are just a little bit impatient like me and need to have all the answers *right now* so you can take immediate action… I do have a quicker solution for you.

You and your team can take the Performance Motivator™ Assessment that I have created to help identify your Performance Motivator™. But… you HAVE TO promise me that you will use it as a start for great conversations with each of these individuals. You've probably already identified which Performance Motivator™ you are, but you might just be surprised once you take the assessment. Sometimes it can be challenging to truly dive in and answer the tough questions. This assessment will test your *true* emotional motivations to uncover that one dominant, deal-breaking Performance Motivator™ that must be satisfied for you—no exceptions.

Take the Performance Motivator Assessment: www.PerformanceMotivator.com or Scan the QR code:

Once you take the assessment, you'll have a much better understanding of yourself.

I encourage you to have your team members take the assessment as well. When they do, take full advantage of this opportunity to have some quality sit-down meetings with each of them to hear what they think, understand them better, and allow it to shape some next-level conversations about how they can bring their best to the workplace in their role and how you can create the path they seek most.

Creating your Signature Culture

Here's where the magic all comes together!

1. You've mastered creating relationships (Structural Footing #1) with everyone, including your own team.

2. You understand the culture you have and the one you want to create—your Company USP. (Structural Footing #2)

3. You and your team are singing its praises from the rooftops.

4. You've completed the exercise of identifying all the ways your culture, missions, and values apply to each of the six Performance Motivators.

5. You understand your competition and where they are lacking, enabling you to identify all the ways you stand out and are unique in the market.

6. You understand your team and what motivates them at their most emotional level—their Performance Motivator™ (Foundation - Performance Motivator System™).

7. Now you can attract, hire, lead, retain, and motivate your team by applying the Performance Motivator System™ (Your Signature Culture) method!

PERFORMANCE MOTIVATOR™ SYSTEM

Once we established our Company USPs, Values, and Mission, notice how the previous Company USP points from Chapter 4 that I mentioned earlier for our company applied to each of the six different Performance Motivators. We didn't change WHO we were to accommodate each of the PMs; we changed how we communicated to each person ABOUT it.

Issues to be solved and how I will communicate…

Growth, learning, and who you can become are available here, not there. *(Success Seeker)*

Your efforts generate tremendous impact for something much greater. *(Impact Player)*

You are taking a big risk there, and while this also has risk, it's far less than the one you're in now. *(Structure Wiz)*

 You can have the balance in life that you have lost recently because that's what we want again too. *(Boundary Balancer)*

 Together we will create a family of people who support each other and create something powerful together. *(Tribe Thinker)*

 We are going to stand for something better than what the industry has already seen; it's time for change and you can be a part of it now to spearhead it with us. *(Change Champion)*

→ Success Seekers like my early self or like many of you may relate to.

→ Impact Players like Clark Kent.

→ Structure Wizzes like Heartwarming Harry.

→ Boundary Balancers like Saint Bonnie.

→ Tribe Thinkers like Boomerang Bob.

→ All the Change Champions who seek "results through meaningful impact."

Having all the information, data, and facts, as well as a clear direction for where you are going, will allow you to shape decisions about positions, roles, salaries, perks, and compensation structure that make sense for your team. You can deliberately choose whether company trips, extra PTO, or a company-paid gym membership will bring the most value to your team. You can structure compensation plans that offer lower salaries but include stock options, incentive bonuses based on goals, or even future buy-out payouts. You can decide whether company picnics, holiday parties, or just extra PTO are the best perks. Instead of offering a long list of expensive and resource-demanding benefits like many companies do, you will have a better understanding of your team's makeup, know the individuals better, and be clear about the Signature Culture that *you* want to create. This will enable you to make decisions that align and connect everything together. You will save money because you chose to make the *right* decisions.

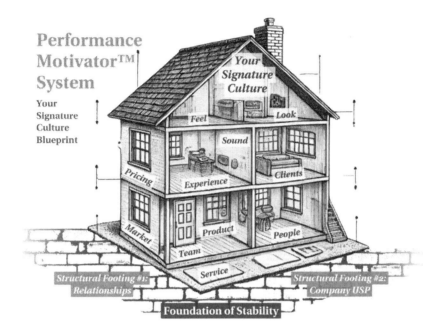

Conclusion

Now you have created YOUR Signature Culture—one that is sought after and desired as the place to work, the place to be. You have created a Best Place to Work in your industry—far above the rest. And it was never about the money.

Why? Because you care. You genuinely care about the culture you create, the company you lead, and the financial strength and future of the organization.

Taking full responsibility for the financial health of your company is your fiscal duty, whether you are an owner or an employee. You have a responsibility to do your part. This impacts the bottom line. This has immeasurable positive effects. A strong company, both financially and culturally, will stand the test of time, continuing to bring success and impact to the world. This is a powerful place to be, and it takes powerful, wise, and strategic leaders to create it. Most won't do it. As much as I wish more would, they won't. This is where the advantage lies for you. You can do it. And when you do, you will be amazed at how you stand out among your peers, your company, and your industry. The advantage you can create will allow you to rise above the rest, and you will be unstoppable.

This is an investment in yourself as a leader. Do you want to be sought after? Do you want to create a loyal following of people who will follow you wherever you go? When you change your career at some point or start that new business, wouldn't it be an incredible asset and value to bring along with you a long list of top talented 'A' players? When you apply the Performance Motivator™ System methods to build your company and the philosophies of

It's Never About the Money, you will see all of these results impact your career too. Your job will be easier when you have trusted, loyal people who want to work hard to create incredible things with you and for you. This is what creates A+ leaders. And hey, the world needs better leaders. There is a *big* shortage! Everywhere you look, there is an opportunity for better leaders. Become that leader, and you will be able to write your own ticket for whatever you want in this world. I know because I've done it. I've both watched and helped others create it. You can create it, too, while also satisfying your core emotional driver, your Performance MotivatorTM. Because *it's never about the money.*

About the Author

Michelle Simms is passionate about creating stronger leaders who can improve organizations, cultures, and relationships for greater impact in the world. Can the world become a better place one leader at a time? Michelle likes to think so.

Following Michelle's successful career and acquisition in the home-building industry, she spent another five years researching and working in the leadership development arena while creating the concepts of this book and the Performance Motivator™ System.

Michelle and her husband, Pablo Reiter, continue to explore their entrepreneurial pursuits through multiple businesses, partnerships, and real estate development projects throughout the Southeast. Most of Michelle's development energy and resources are focused on those partnerships to help companies create their own Signature Culture, find operational efficiencies, and develop leaders to scale their businesses to the next level. Michelle and Pablo continue to invest and partner with those businesses that are the right match. If you are interested in a partnership opportunity in your business, or to learn more about Michelle, you can find more details and explore possibilities by visiting her website at: www.MichelleSimmsReiter.com to get to know her better and allow her to do the same.

When they are not working hard creating successful businesses, Michelle and Pablo love to travel, golf, boat, and live life to the fullest with their three kids and two dogs in Raleigh, NC.

Resources

You can find the Performance Motivator Assessment™ here: www.PerformanceMotivator.com

More about the Author: www.MichelleSimmsReiter.com

Acknowledgments

My Terramor family will always remain a huge piece of my heart. From our early days and very humble beginnings, we learned and grew together to build and create something special, something we all hungered for and then held dear, caring for it once we did, and as we continued to grow. We raised our children together, we loved our pets together, we celebrated some of the most monumental aspects of our lives together, and we supported each other in our losses and pain—together. "Together is better" defined us and made us stronger. You each inspired me to grow and become a better leader for you. You required more of me each day, with love, and I was eager to bring it. You taught me how to become a better version of myself. I appreciate each of you for that. I only hope I was able to give back to you in these ways or to others who have impacted your lives and left a mark on you as well. You are each special to me—you always will be—and watching you continue to grow and create further, bigger, more incredible opportunities for yourselves brings me a pride and joy that is unlike anything else I can compare it to in life—the closest being the pride of watching your kids become successful and do great things. So thank you. Thank you for bringing the best of yourselves, and thank you for making me do the same. Our children will forever be able to tell the stories of growing up, being inspired by each of you from their earliest ages, and being welcomed, entertained, taught, and most importantly, *loved* by each of you. For that, I am eternally grateful from the bottom of my heart.

To Pablo: you became my partner in business long before you became my partner in life. You entrusted me at a time when the stakes were high. You brought patience as I learned to become the business owner I knew I could be, and you supported and respected me as a woman leader from the very start. Our earliest days and some of our biggest life struggles were experienced during these times, as were some of our greatest celebrations and milestones for personal growth. I'm proud of the work we've done, and I'm blown away by what we were able to create together with the Terramor family and beyond. Creating two families at the same time—our Terramor tribe and our family at home, which in many ways are one—was one of the most challenging yet gratifying experiences of my life. We could never have planned any of the events that transpired over these 10+ years, which is difficult for two controlling people! But I guess that's one of the lessons in all of this: some things we just can't plan; life takes over and does it for us. There's so much more that lies ahead, and I'm proud you are my partner in it all. Thank you for challenging me, and thank you for your constant support and belief in me. You make me better.

To Jensen, Julian, and Gaby: While we didn't see it at the time, looking back, I know that this slice of time was one of the most impactful in your lives. When I think through all of the memories and experiences that happened— the good and the bad—I know that it all had a big purpose. It was filled with so much love and support. It shaped your lives and influenced who you have become. You each have everything you need in life, and this time and these people were a big part of that. You are so fortunate to have had them all. We are so proud of you and couldn't be more excited to watch you follow your dreams and create your big futures too. Thank you for being such incredible people and for inspiring us to be better each day for you too. We love each of you more than you know.

Countless other friends, family, mentors, peers and bosses have supported, taught, advised and guided me throughout my life and I will be forever grateful for each of them- thank you!

THANK YOU FOR READING MY BOOK!

Take the Assessment

AND

Gain Free Access to More Resources

Take the Quiz:

I appreciate your interest in my book and value your feedback as it helps me improve future versions of this book. I would appreciate it if you could leave your invaluable review on Amazon.com with your feedback. Thank you!

Made in the USA
Middletown, DE
01 April 2025

73522641R00092